Nuclear War, Nuclear Winter

NUCLEAR WAR,

NUCLEAR WINTER

Gene B. Williams

Franklin Watts
New York / London
Toronto / Sydney / 1987
An Impact Book

Photographs courtesy of Naval Photographic Center,
Official U.S. Navy Photograph: pp. 13, 79;
UPI/Bettmann Newsphotos: pp. 19, 38, 68, 92
(Reuters); United Nations: p. 25; The Bettmann
Archive, Inc.: pp. 34, 45; NASA: p.37; U.S. Forest
Service: p. 50; Photo Researchers, Inc.: pp. 62
(Horace Bristol, Jr.), 83 (Julian Baum/Science
Photo Library); USDA: p. 73; U.S. Air Force Photo:
p. 88; Museum of the City of New York: p. 100.

Library of Congress Cataloging-in-Publication Data

Williams, Gene B.
Nuclear war, nuclear winter.

(An Impact book)
Bibliography: p.
Includes index.
Summary: Discusses the history, weapons, and
probable effects of nuclear warfare, as well as
the dangers of global extinction and possible alternatives.
  1. Nuclear warfare—Juvenile literature.
  2. Nuclear winter—Juvenile literature. 3. Arms
race—History—20th century—Juvenile literature.
[1. Nuclear warfare. 2. Nuclear winter]
I. Title.
U263.W55   1987   355'.0217   87–8337
                          ISBN 0–531–10416–8

Contents

Nuclear War, Nuclear Winter

1

Nuclear Winter

Right in the middle of your favorite television program the screen goes blank, and the whine of the Emergency Broadcast System follows. Only this time it's not a test. The missiles are coming. For whatever reason, World War III has begun and there's not a thing you can do about it.

Off in the distance you can see the vapor trails of our own missiles leaving their silos, heading toward targets on the other side of the world before the incoming weapons can destroy and make useless those silos. The trails are criss-crossed in the sky by the trails of jets. If the television, radio, or telephones were still working, you'd find out that the same scene is being played all across the nation.

It's too late to wonder why, or to ask who pushed the button first. It doesn't really matter anyway. You have less than twenty minutes to wonder about those things—twenty precious minutes to do whatever you can to survive.

And then time runs out.

The noise and heat and wind are awesome. Even though you are miles away from the actual target, the force is sufficient to cause damage to your house and your neighbors' houses. You can hear a portion of your house being torn away. The odor of smoke creeps into your hiding spot.

Some time later you gather together your courage and crawl outside. It's raining—not drops of water but dust and debris. There are several small fires scattered around the neighborhood, but no water to fight them, nor is there likely to be any. All services and utilities are gone. All you can get from the faucets is a tiny trickle from what remains in the pipes.

In the distance you can see the firestorms raging through the city, with huge clouds of black smoke pouring into the air so heavily that it's difficult to see, and almost as difficult to breathe. Toxic fumes from the firestorm cause your breath to come in choking gasps.

You look at your watch. It says 7:13. But is that AM or PM? Your sense of time is mixed up. It should be morning, but it's dark enough to be evening.

Will the firestorm brought on by the nuclear blasts come in your direction? How much radiation from the blasts did you absorb? Is there enough food and water in the house to keep you alive long enough for help to arrive? Will help arrive at all? How many people survived the attack?

The days pass. The firestorm in the city has burned itself out at last, but you almost wish that there was some fire because it's starting to get cold. The sun has all but disappeared. Day, night—there doesn't seem to be much difference. Sun, moon, and stars can't be seen through that thick blanket of dust and smoke.

The low-level smoke and dust settle out of the air in a few weeks. The upper atmosphere is still hazy, and the haze still blocks the sun. The temperature continues to drop until it is well below freezing. The trees and plants are dying, both from the cold and from the lack of sunlight needed for photosynthesis.

You've survived the initial attack. You may even survive several months of subfreezing temperatures (despite the fact that it's mid-July). Not much else will.

The innermost portions of the country are hit the worst, with some areas suffering from drops in temperature of as much as 144°F (80°C). The coastal areas are kept warmer by the heat stored in the oceans, but this is a mixed blessing. The difference in temperature between the inland areas and the coast is causing hurricane-force winds which tear away at the few remaining structures.

Those who live south of the equator, where fewer weapons exploded, are spared, but only for a few weeks. The clouds swing southward. By the end of the first month, the amount of sunlight reaching the surface has greatly decreased virtually everywhere on earth. Darker, heavier clouds over the target areas throw these into an almost perpetual night, possibly for months to come.

Until fairly recently, the accepted scenario for an all-out nuclear war was this: about 1 billion people would be killed immediately and another billion or so would die in the following months from radiation, disease, starvation, and a host of other effects. Even so, it was assumed that a third to a half of the population of the United States and the Soviet Union (assuming these are the primary adversaries) could survive, with the population of the Southern Hemisphere suffering much less. Some estimates place the survival rate even higher, some place it lower.

These estimates are based on the effect of individual nuclear blasts, not on the combined effects of a major exchange. In the case of multiple detonations, the death rate will be much higher, perhaps even to the point of extinction of the human race.

In October 1983, a group of scientists gathered for the "Conference on the World After Nuclear War." In a research paper at this meeting, "Global Atmospheric

Consequences of Nuclear War," the TTAPS Model was presented. The initials stand for the scientists who developed the model—Richard P. Turco, O. Brian Toon, Thomas P. Ackerman, James B. Pollack, and Carl Sagan. Turco coined the term that is now commonly used to describe the aftermath of nuclear war: "nuclear winter."

Nuclear winter is a bleak picture of our world after even a relatively minor nuclear exchange. According to the findings of the TTAPS group and others, billions of tons of dust, soot, and ash could be tossed into the atmosphere, accompanied by smoke and poisonous fumes from the firestorms.

The TTAPS model indicates that, in the case of a severe exchange, within a few days the entire Northern Hemisphere could be under a blanket so thick that as little as one-tenth of one percent of normal sunlight would reach the earth. The more "generous" findings list sunlight blockage at 95 percent, with 5 percent of normal sunlight reaching the ground.

Without sunlight, temperatures will fall, just as they do at night. But this time, the "night" could last for months. Interior regions, according to the studies, could drop well below freezing and stay there for a year and possibly longer.

Those who survive the initial attack could be facing an even longer period before plants could grow again. According to one study, there would be major crop failure that would last for years. Without crops, there is nothing to eat. Nor can you just switch to eating nothing but meat for a few years. Even the animals won't have food, and will starve.

After a nuclear war, the world could look like this scene of Hiroshima after the atom bomb was dropped.

An even more important plant would also die out. Microscopic plants that are part of the plankton in the oceans are at the base of both the food chain and the oxygen cycle. Just as the more immediately edible plants inland will die without sunlight, so will the plankton in the ocean. Destroy the plankton and you also destroy a major portion of the food chain. And as oxygen-producing plants die off, it's going to get difficult to breathe after a while.

One of the panelists at the "Conference on the World After Nuclear War" stated that the winner of a nuclear World War III would be the winner for only about two weeks. After this, even if the first strike totally disables the attacked and no retaliation is possible, nuclear winter will destroy the attacker.

The thought of half of the world's population dying in a war is frightening enough. Worse, we could actually be facing global extinction. This is what the nuclear-winter theorists predict. Ultimately, in an arms race there can be no winner.

2

A Brief History of the Arms Race

Depending on your point of view, World War II officially began either in 1939 with the German invasion of Poland, or in 1941 when the Japanese attacked Pearl Harbor and the United States entered the war. It ended in late 1945 with the surrender of Japan, after the introduction of a devastating new weapon.

Just a few days prior to the signing of the surrender, the world was given a practical demonstration of this new weapon—the atomic bomb.

The theories of nuclear fission—the splitting of atoms and the consequent release of energy—have been around since the early 1900s. In 1939 Albert Einstein sent a letter to the president, Franklin Roosevelt, which discussed the possibilities of a weapon using fission.

On December 2, 1942, a team headed by the physicist Enrico Fermi brought about the first nuclear chain reaction, using the isotope U-235. This was followed almost immediately by the development of the Manhattan Project, with its base in Los Alamos, New Mexico.

The results of this project were first demonstrated on July 16, 1945. On the desert of White Sands near Alamogordo, New Mexico, the world's first atomic bomb was set off.

The next atomic explosion had a more military function. On August 6, 1945, Hiroshima was bombed. The bomb, called "Little Boy," was a mere 10 feet (3 meters) in length and 2 feet 4 inches (7 decimeters) in diameter. It had the explosive force equivalent of 13 kilotons (13 thousand tons, or 26 million pounds) of TNT. Three-fifths of the city's population—100,000 people—were killed and more than half the city was destroyed.

Three days later the "Fat Man" (just 8 inches, or 20 centimeters, longer than "Little Boy" but with twice the diameter) was dropped on Nagasaki. Less than a week after this, Japan, threatened with more such bombings, agreed to the terms of an unconditional surrender.

The Arms Race Begins

Along with the end of World War II came the beginning of what is known as the Cold War and also the beginning of the nuclear arms race.

Those first atom bombs, although firecrackers compared to the weapons of today, frightened the world so much that efforts were made to outlaw any further research or development. In June 1946, the United Nations Atomic Energy Commission took the first steps to prohibit nuclear weapons.

The Soviet Union rejected the plan outright, saying that it would leave the United States as the only country with such weapons. Their stand against the ban was further strengthened when the United States exploded yet another atom bomb over the Bikini Atoll in the Pacific Ocean on July 1, 1946—just days after presentation of the proposal that would outlaw such tests.

Within three years the Soviet Union had developed atom bombs of their own, exploding their first in 1949.

Meanwhile, the United States continued its own research for bigger and better weapons. In 1952, just seven years after the first atom bombs destroyed Hiroshima and Nagasaki, the world was to be astounded once again. This time the testing ground was the Eniwetok Atoll. The device tested was the first hydrogen bomb. The power of this bomb, 10.4 megatons (10.4 million tons), the equivalent of some 800 Hiroshima bombs, vaporized a fair portion of the island target.

This time the Soviets were only ten months behind U.S. nuclear technology. Less than a year later, in 1953, the Soviets exploded their own first H-bomb.

Toward the end of World War II, Germany had introduced their own new weapons, the robot "buzz-bombs" of the V-1 and V-2 rockets. These rockets were used to deliver explosive warheads (non-nuclear) to targets hundreds of miles away. England was a primary target. Many feel that if Germany had developed these rockets earlier, the outcome of the war would have been different.

After the end of the war (and even before), many of Germany's top scientists fled to the United States. Through the 1950s, rocketry research continued. By 1958 the space race was coupled to the nuclear arms race. With more and more powerful rockets being constructed, satellites placed into orbit became common news. Rocket engines also made it possible to drop nuclear warheads on targets many thousands of miles away from the launching site—even across the entire globe.

During the 1950s relations between the United States and the Soviet Union continued to worsen. To forestall a possible attack by the Soviets on Western Europe, the United States began to deploy nuclear weapons throughout the "friendly" nations of Europe until about 7,000 such weapons were armed and ready.

Toward the end of the 1950s, the Soviets responded by installing a number of SS-4 and SS-5 intermediate range weapons, each carrying a 1-megaton warhead, aimed at key targets in Europe.

Treaties

In November 1958 Great Britain, the United States, and the Soviet Union agreed to stop nuclear testing. This moratorium lasted until September 1961, when France began to conduct nuclear testing in the atmosphere. The Soviets claimed that because France was a NATO ally of the United States and Great Britain, the moratorium had been violated. Atmospheric testing was carried out in full force for the next few years.

Through the 1960s the world faced several incidents that threatened a war. For example, to counter the threat of U.S. missiles based along Soviet borders, the Soviet Union began installation of nuclear weapons in Cuba. This precipitated the Cuban Missile Crisis in 1963, and brought the world to the brink of World War III.

Negotiations defused the situation, and also produced the Limited Test Ban Treaty. This once again brought an end to nuclear testing in the atmosphere, but allowed underground testing to continue.

This treaty is still in effect, with 123 countries around the world participating. Of the major nuclear powers of the world, only France and China have refused to sign, although France has ceased above-ground testing.

Until the first moratorium in 1958, there were about 250 testings in the atmosphere. Since the LTB Treaty of 1963 went into effect, the United States has conducted about 400 underground tests, and the Soviets conducting about 300.

Nuclear Power

The entire explosive force expended in World War II was equal to 2 megatons of TNT; this is 2 million tons, or 4,000,000,000,000 (4 trillion) pounds of dynamite. Try to imagine what a single pound of dynamite would do to you or your home and you'll have an idea of the

Four GIs read with pleasure the news of the defusing of the Cuban Missile Crisis in October 1962.

amount of explosive power expended during World War II. This force was spread out, however, over a period of about six years.

As mentioned, "Little Boy" had the power of 13 kilotons. In a single step the power rating of a bomb jumped from a thousand pounds of explosive to millions of pounds. About a year later, improvements had been made to allow for a 20-kiloton explosive. The next step, the H-bomb, brought a piece of the sun to earth, with power rated in the millions of tons. (To equal the power of the first H-bomb, you'd have to set off simultaneously, and all in one place, 20 billion pounds of TNT. This is like bundling up all the explosive power of five World War IIs, and setting it all off within a second.)

An average nuclear weapon today has that much power, and more. A 2- to 3-megaton warhead is about standard. Bombs with explosive power of 5 or 10 megatons are common.

As you read this, there are somewhere between 55,000 and 60,000 nuclear weapons in existence. By tomorrow there will be at least ten more. Of these, nearly 20,000 are "strategic," which means that they are designed to go from one country, across the ocean, to strike another country. Any one of these is powerful enough to destroy an entire large city.

Many of the nuclear weapons are landbased. As such, these are especially vulnerable to attack. If a bomb strikes a silo field, the missiles stored there cannot be launched easily, if at all. Assuming the worst—an attack coming in unnoticed and totally disabling all ground defenses and offenses—another possible defense has been supplied.

The United States alone has thirty submarines on patrol equipped with nuclear weaponry. These submarines are almost immune to attack. Each has sufficient nuclear warheads on board to destroy between 150 and 200 cities. Even with all landbased weapons gone, the U.S. submarine force is capable of annihilating 4,500 to

6,000 cities. Just three of these submarines can destroy more cities than exist in the Soviet Union. In fact, in 1979 President Carter stated, "Just one of our relatively invulnerable Poseidon submarines—less than 2 percent of our total nuclear force of submarines, aircraft, and landbased missiles—carries enough warheads to destroy every large and medium-sized city in the Soviet Union." The Soviet Union has a similar destructive potential.

Our world has gradually built up a vast stockpile of weapons. It has been calculated that there is now the equivalent of approximately four tons of TNT for every man, woman, and child on earth. It has been predicted that, if the arms race continues at its present rate, in ten years that amount will at least double.

As the number and power of warheads increase, so does the technology used to deliver those warheads to their respective targets. "Little Boy" was delivered by a bomber as it flew over its target. Although the effects of that blast were considerable, the accuracy was somewhat lacking.

Today, from a distance of up to 4,000 miles (6,436 kilometers) missiles and guidance systems can deliver a warhead to within 450 yards (410 meters). Newer and better guidance systems are under development with a predicted targeting accuracy of within 55 yards (50 meters) from as far away as 6,000 miles (9,650 kilometers).

3

Single Warhead Studies

According to the World Health Organization, a large-scale nuclear war could immediately kill over 1 billion people. Another billion or so could die from the side-effects of such a war—radiation, epidemic disease, starvation, and so on. Thus, a nuclear war could result in the deaths of between 2 and 3 billion people, even before considering the possible effects of nuclear winter.

An estimate developed by the Office of Technology Assessment (OTA) in 1979 predicts that up to 73 percent of the American population could die as an immediate result of a nuclear war. This study does not take into account the deaths occurring after the holocaust, even from such "normal" problems as radiation, lack of medical care, and war-related serious injuries.

Until recently such figures were calculated only on the effects of single warhead blasts. And except for just two cases (Hiroshima and Nagasaki), all available information on the effects comes from test-controlled detonations.

The First Explosions

The first actual studies of the effects of a nuclear explosion were made possible by the detonation of bombs over Hiroshima and Nagasaki near the end of World War II. Even scientists didn't know quite what the results would be. The studies were incomplete. Even so, certain things are known.

The temperature of a nuclear explosion reaches into the millions of degrees. "Little Boy," exploded 1,000 feet (300 meters) above Hiroshima, caused the surface temperature to jump to well over 5,000 degrees almost instantly. Citizens more than two miles (3 kilometers) from the blast were burned.

The force of the explosion annihilated everything within more than a mile of the center. Photographs were taken showing where "shadows" had been burned into concrete walls; the humans who were the sources of the shadows had been completely vaporized.

It has been estimated that nearly 60 percent of the population of Hiroshima died either instantly or within a few weeks. Many more died later. Even today, more than forty years after explosion, the effects are still showing up. The children of the survivors continue to carry the "radioactive plague."

Yet "Little Boy" was very small compared to the warheads presently available.

OTA and Other Studies

The OTA study in 1979 released the predicted results of more modern nuclear warhead blasts. The city of Detroit, Michigan, was used as a prime example of what could happen in an area of high population density.

If a single 1-megaton warhead exploded at ground level, it would kill 220,000 people and injure another

An atomic cloud bursting over Hiroshima two minutes after the explosion on August 6, 1945

420,000. If this same warhead was detonated in the air, the immediate death toll would be 470,000 and another 630,000 would sustain injuries.

The same attack with a single 25-megaton warhead would obviously produce greater results. An airburst of such a warhead would almost instantly kill 1,840,000 and injure another 1,360,000.

Neither set of statistics includes those who would die later from injuries or from radioactive fallout. They merely give an indication of the death rate immediately (within thirty days) following a nuclear attack on that city. It has been predicted that the number of deaths could easily be doubled when all other side effects are taken into account.

As to physical damage to the city, the report stated that a single 1-megaton warhead would create a crater 200 feet (60 meters) deep and 1,000 feet (300 meters) wide, with a radioactive "shell" extending out to about 2,000 feet (600 meters). All buildings within a two-mile (three-kilometer) radius of the explosion would be utterly destroyed, and there would be few or no survivors.

For the next mile (between two and three miles, or three and five kilometers, from the center of the explosion) very few buildings would remain standing. Most would collapse from overpressure, killing anyone inside.

From three to five miles (five to eight kilometers) away, standard houses would be destroyed along with many heavier structures. Virtually all buildings would sustain damage.

Beyond the five-mile (eight-kilometer) radius, only about one fourth of the population would be killed instantly. Many would suffer from severe burns, both from the blast and from massive fires that resulted from the explosion.

Physicians for Social Responsibility ran calculations

of their own on the effects of a single 20-megaton war-head on a densely populated area. This group used Boston as its example. The estimates showed almost total destruction of the city and casualties of at least 1.5 million. They went on to say that the number of deaths would be increased by the lack of medical care and resources caused by an almost total destruction of such facilities.

The above study and several others have predicted that, although the force of the blast will cause severe damage, even more destruction and deaths will result from the thermal radiation (heat), the subsequent firestorms, the immediate radiation, and later the radioactive fallout.

In a report in the *Bulletin of Atomic Scientists* Bernard Feld said that a nuclear war would most likely escalate quickly, with some 5,000 megatons falling on the United States. According to this report, potentially serious levels of radioactive fallout would cover an area equal to more than 5 million square miles. This is about one and a half times the area of the United States.

Depending on the winds at the time, this fallout would probably be spread out over a larger area, and thus reduce the number of deaths. Even so, such a major nuclear exchange would probably create enough fallout to affect every living thing in the United States.

At the beginning of this nuclear age, the total effects of fallout were unknown. Between 1946 and 1963 many open-air tests were performed. The effects of the fallout began to show up in increased rates of cancer in affected towns. Strontium-90 was found in the milk of cows thousands of miles away from the test site.

In 1963 the dangers were well enough known to cause the signing of a test-ban treaty. This treaty greatly restricted above-ground tests in the world, and also reduced the amount of fallout.

Radiation and Fallout

In theory scientists knew that a nuclear explosion would cause surrounding materials to carry and hold radiation. This was shown to be the case after the first atomic test. The truth of it became more dramatic in Hiroshima and Nagasaki. So, even at the very beginning of the nuclear age, the fact that radioactive fallout would reach out and kill far beyond the epicenter of the explosion was known and understood.

Science fiction writers took up the idea and began to create doomsday stories. Hollywood filled the movie theaters with films showing mutated and deadly beasts formed as a result of radioactivity.

In 1957 Nevil Shute wrote a novel, *On the Beach,* which two years later was made into a movie. The story was about a submarine crew based in Australia when the United States and the Soviet Union get into a major nuclear war. No one is left alive in the United States. A cloud of radioactive dust moves out and covers the earth. Australia is the last place on earth where humans are still alive, waiting for death as the cloud moves toward Australia.

Finally there is a frightening scene of a town square with no people, just some newspapers blowing in the wind. (We now know that such a scene would be highly unlikely—at least, clouds of radioactivity probably would not be enough to cause such a scene.)

The destructive power of a nuclear blast is well documented. From hundreds of tests performed over the years, scientists know how much pressure and heat will be released in the explosion. From this data the number of people killed, the number of buildings destroyed, and the amount of lesser damage can be calculated with fair accuracy.

From there the estimates become less certain. Radioactive fallout would be responsible for many deaths over the next year and more. Just where this fallout lands, and how many people it affects, would depend on the weather. How fast is the wind blowing, and in which direction? How much rain is there to help wash out the radioactive particles? How far up into the atmosphere have these particles traveled?

The secondary killing effect of radiation depends on the dosage received. Radiation dose is measured in rems. A dose of between 250 and 400 rems over a period of 7 days will kill 50 percent of the victims, and will injure more.

That 1-megaton blast would generate 3,000 rems over a radius of 50 miles. The length of time this dose would be present would depend once again on the weather and other prevailing conditions.

The problem with trying to predict what would actually happen after a major nuclear war is that there is no solid information available. Only twice has a nuclear weapon been used in war. And when those explosions occurred over Hiroshima and Nagasaki nobody knew quite what to expect, especially concerning the after-effects.

Special hospitals have been set up in both towns to take care of the *hibakusha* ("bomb-affected people"). The hospitals are not only to care for these people, but also to attempt to discover more about the effects of a nuclear blast.

So far, only indications are available. It is known that the average person receives just slightly over one tenth of a rad per year from the normal radioactivity level of our planet. One rad is equal to 1 billion particles per square centimeter. Survivors of Hiroshima and Nagasaki received an average of fifteen to twenty rads. Many were exposed to levels of 100 rads and more. Most of those who were contaminated with 400 rads or more have died.

The studies show a greatly increased rate of cancer.

Leukemia began to show up among the survivors just two years after the studies began. The indications are that among those who received 100 rads the rate of leukemia is 20 times (2,000%) greater than it is among the general population. Also found among the victims are higher rates of multiple myeloma (including bone marrow disease) and a large variety of other ills.

According to the best estimates available, radiation killed 200,000 within the first 3 months, and another 140,000 over the next 5 years.

The bomb used on Hiroshima was based on U-235; the Nagasaki bomb was a plutonium-239 device. The uranium-based bomb gave off greater amounts of neutron radiation, while the bomb dropped on Nagasaki had higher levels of gamma radiation. Differences between the two have been studied.

Nothing conclusive has resulted as yet. The indications are that those affected by neutron radiation have a slightly higher rate of cancer than those from Nagasaki. However, Dr. David Hoel, director of the group in charge of aiding recovery, has said that new information points to a risk 50 percent higher than previously anticipated. He further points out that the full effects of the radiation contamination may not appear for another fifteen years or so.

Beyond the continuing studies of the survivors of Hiroshima and Nagasaki, very little information is available—or even possible to obtain.

Heat, Firestorms,
and Electromagnetism

Approximately one third of the total energy released by a nuclear explosion comes as heat. The small atom bomb over Hiroshima flashed with a temperature of millions of degrees. The more modern and more powerful warheads of today produce even higher temperatures.

At the moment of detonation, a temperature of up to about 21,000,000°F (about 11,500,000°C) will occur. As the explosion continues, energy spreads out. The temperature decreases, and X rays are emitted. By the time a typical airburst detonation touches the ground, the temperature has dropped to about 21,000°F (11,500°C). Virtually anything the superheated air touches will ignite.

Massive fires begin. As the attacked city burns, the individual fires join. Then, fed by violent convection currents, they become a firestorm that could sweep through what remains of the city.

To make matters worse, in most cities there is an abundance of chemicals, plastics, and other materials that give off poisonous fumes while burning. These are called pyrotoxins. The amount released depends on the target, the number of individual fires, and the extent (or existence) of a firestorm.

Many of the targets are not cities but are more rural areas. Crops or forests near the explosion will be instantly destroyed. If a condition of dryness is present, those fires, too, will spread.

Our society exists as a complex web. Each of the parts becomes a part of the greater whole by staying in communication with all other parts. The military is even more vulnerable to communications breakdowns. If the generals and strategists can't communicate with the troops in the field, the battle at hand can be more easily lost.

Today much of the communication takes place along telephone lines and radio waves. The equipment needed for this is electronic. The components inside the equipment are, by nature, sensitive to electromagnetism.

A 1-megaton blast 100 kilometers (62 miles) up could send an electromagnetic pulse to the ground with a force of some 25,000 volts per square meter (roughly equivalent to a square yard). This doesn't mean that you will be getting a shock. It does mean that almost any delicate electronic circuit could be destroyed. Communications then break down except in those sites that have been "hardened" to protect the equipment from the electromagnetic blast that accompanies the nuclear blast.

Even if there were any radio stations still on the air after a nuclear war, your radio wouldn't be able to pick them up. The electronic circuits would have been destroyed.

The Problem with the Studies

Nuclear-winter theorists say that while previous studies show the incredible devastation of a nuclear war, they fail to show the combined effects of hundreds, or thousands, of such warheads exploding almost simultaneously.

They point to the amount of dust that would be raised by a nuclear explosion. Tests indicate that approximately three metric tons per megaton of explosive will be lifted into the stratosphere. Of this, about 8 percent could remain in the atmosphere for a year or longer.

Additionally, projectors of nuclear winter claim that somewhere between 1 percent and 6 percent of the smoke and soot from the fires on the surface will reach into the upper atmosphere.

Although 8 percent of the dust and about 4 percent (accepted as an average by several sources) of the smoke and soot do not seem like much, there is little argument even among the more optimistic, that this would be sufficient to greatly reduce the amount of sunlight. This could result in greatly reduced temperatures on the surface.

But will a major exchange cause this much dust, smoke, and soot to get into the atmosphere, and then stay there long enough to cause a serious problem?

4

Accidental Discoveries

Even before there were nuclear weapons there have been individuals and groups who have lobbied and otherwise fought against these weapons. Among them was Albert Einstein, sometimes known as the Father of the Nuclear Age.

Until recently, these groups could only point to the massive devastation possible with nuclear weapons, and to the horrible deaths from radiation poisoning. Several studies showed that it would be entirely possible for half of the people on earth to lose their lives in a major confrontation.

Then, beginning in the early 1970s, several discoveries were made that originally seemed unrelated to the topic of nuclear war.

Studies of Another World

In late 1971 the Mariner 9 probe went into orbit around Mars. To the disappointment of those monitoring the probe back on Earth, pictures and other readings of the surface of the planet were impossible. A planet-wide windstorm was sweeping over Mars—the entire surface of the planet was obscured.

*Albert Einstein, German-born
American physicist, laid the groundwork
for the harnessing of atomic energy.*

Unlike Earth, Mars has a very thin atmosphere. Wind on that planet has a much greater effect on the surface dust. And that dust is made all the more prominent because the surface and atmosphere of Mars are almost completely without water. When a heavy wind blows, a tremendous amount of dust is lifted into the atmosphere, and at heights that would be impossible on earth.

Temperature readings taken by Mariner 9 showed that the upper atmosphere of Mars was much warmer than usual, while the surface was much colder.

Eventually the windstorm stopped and the atmosphere began to clear. The readings taken by Mariner's instruments showed the change in temperature in the atmosphere and on the surface. The changes were far greater than expected.

It was determined that the cause of the unusual temperature shifts was the dust storm. The dust had absorbed and reflected much of the incoming sunlight, causing the atmosphere to become warmer than usual, and the surface to become considerably cooler.

It took quite a few months before the temperatures returned to normal again. Meanwhile, the scientific team that made the study was able to calculate the amount of dust that had been in the atmosphere and to compare this with the significant drop in temperature on the surface. The results of these calculations were the beginnings of the theory of nuclear winter.

Many people assume incorrectly that a planet hidden beneath a heavy cover would automatically exhibit the "Greenhouse Effect." The combined effects of clouds and a planet's atmosphere, however, are more complicated.

On Earth, a few clouds in the atmosphere help to keep things cool. There are breaks in the clouds that allow heat to escape. A more solid cloud cover, such as the one that blanketed Mars in 1971, will cause more shadowing of the planet below. The thin atmosphere of

Mars cannot hold heat. Thus, at least initially, the temperature drops.

When an atmosphere is present, however, those same clouds over a period of many years could have the opposite effect. Just as they reflect heat and sunlight back into space, they reflect heat and light back to the planet. The atmosphere absorbs the heat, and the temperature climbs. An example of this would be Venus, which has a heavy cloud cover and a dense atmosphere (primarily carbon dioxide). Due to this effect, Venus is considerably hotter than Mercury, despite its greater distance from the sun.

Studies made by Soviet scientists seem to indicate that a nuclear winter—the sudden drop in temperature—will be followed by a "nuclear summer."

In 1976 Viking II landed on Mars. Photographs of the surface showed drifts of the fine dust that had been the cause of the dust storm five years before. Additional tests confirmed information relayed by Mariner 9. The inescapable conclusion was that a cloud of dust, on Mars or elsewhere, would cause the temperature on the surface to plummet.

Back on Earth

Brian Toon of NASA began studying volcanoes and their effects on climate. After seeing the results of the dust storms on Mars, he theorized that perhaps the same thing could happen on earth—not from dust storms, but from dust, smoke, soot, and ash tossed into the air by volcanic activity or other forces. He saw "an interesting parallel between Mars and the earth."

In May 1980, Mount St. Helens erupted, throwing a quarter of a cubic mile of dust and ash into the air. The winds carried this dense cover over the town of Yakima in south central Washington. This small town was thrown into almost complete darkness at noon as the ash blocked out the sunlight.

*In this photograph taken by Mariner 9,
Mars shines dimly through clouds of dust.
The dust absorbs and reflects sunlight,
making the planet surface very cold.*

*Studying the effects of volcanic eruptions,
like this one at Mount St. Helens in
1980, helps scientists predict the effects
of nuclear-weapon explosions.*

This effect was localized downwind from the eruption. Within a short time, the particles came out of the atmosphere by various natural forces. As powerful as was the eruption, almost all of the particles stayed within the troposphere, where normal weather can act upon them and remove them in a relatively short time.

Just two years later, in April 1982, another volcanic eruption occurred in southern Mexico. El Chichon in the province of Chiapas erupted, killing more than 200 people in the village below. This time the plumes of dust and ash were photographed and tracked steadily by satellite. It took three weeks for it to circle the earth.

For the next couple of years, the major visible effects of the eruption were the change in color of the sunsets and the appearance of a whitish ring around the sun. Both were caused as the particles scattered the incoming sunlight.

Effects on the climate were much less pronounced. The change in climate was too small for scientists to point conclusively to the volcanic eruption as the cause. However, many claimed that the changes in the weather in 1982 and 1983 were brought about by this volcano.

While the dust and ash from Mount St. Helens came out of the atmosphere quickly, the results of El Chichon were more long-lasting. The force of the eruption was considerably greater, and the clouds of material were tossed far into the stratosphere.

The troposphere has the effects of weather to clean away particles. The stratosphere has no weather, as we think of it. Particles in the stratosphere tend to stay there for much longer periods of time.

Volcanoes in History

The findings from the results of these two volcanic eruptions were combined in new studies that showed correlation of frost damage to volcanic activity.

One of the first correlations involved the 1815 eruption of Tambora in Indonesia. The following year, 1816, was known as "The Year Without a Summer," and was well documented. The immediate after effect was a global decrease in temperature of 1.8°F (1°C). As minor as this might seem, the eruption has been linked to major changes that occurred in the weather throughout the world. For example, an epidemic of cholera in India and Persia that began in 1815 and lasted for almost twenty years was traced to changes in weather caused by the eruption of Tambora. As far away as New England in the United States, it snowed in June of 1816.

Intrigued by the effects of volcanic dust clouds on the climate, and the resultant effects, Michael Kelly of the University of East Anglia in Great Britain began attempts to make a historical correlation.

He correlated the average daily temperatures around the world with six of the major volcanic eruptions in recent history. The temperature readings recorded during the years immediately following the eruptions were averaged to reduce the effects of normal climate variations. These averages were then compared to normal averages for other years in order to get an accurate picture of the effects of various eruptions on the overall climate of our planet.

This study showed that the average global temperature after a major eruption dropped as much as 1.8°F (1°C) within a month or so after the eruption, and stayed lower than normal for a long period.

The greatest temperature changes were over the continental landmass interiors. The warming effects of the oceans were also decreased, making coastal areas colder than usual at these times.

A study conducted by the University of Arizona found a way to look at the effects of historical eruptions. The subject of this study was the bristlecone pine trees found in California. Some of these trees are known to be more than 4,000 years old, thus being some of the oldest living things on earth.

Core samples were taken so that the seasonal growth rings could be examined under a microscope. A number of the rings showed frost damage, caused by temperatures that were colder than normal during a particular growth cycle. This could be explained by variations in the local or global climate.

The width and other characteristics of these rings were then charted and correlated to known major volcanic eruptions around the world. The correlation of frost damage to major eruptions in history was nearly perfect. Within a few months to about a year after each major eruption over the past several thousand years, the climate had been changed even thousands of miles away.

This seemed to demonstrate that global temperature drops had been caused by major eruptions down through history. Additional core samples were taken from other trees from areas all over the world. Again the growth rings, and the frost damage shown by those rings, were charted. They compared to the earlier findings.

What the Studies Mean

The studies of Mars and its dust storm and particularly of the volcanic activity on Earth and the effects on the climate showed two important things.

First, something that happens in one place can indeed affect the climate of an entire planet. The dust storm on Mars was worldwide and dense. It brought with it a large decrease in temperature on the surface of the planet.

The amount of dust tossed into the atmosphere of Earth from a volcanic eruption is considerably less than was present on Mars during the dust storm. Movements in the atmosphere spread the dust out until it is just barely visible. Even so, it can create a sufficient decrease in the global temperature to cause damage to growth.

The second important point is that it takes only a small change in the overall climate for the effects to be noticed. A temperature decrease of as little as one degree will cause damage. A change of several degrees can cause a disaster.

5

---

*Extinction of
a Species*

The idea that dust and clouds can block the sun, and thus reduce the surface temperature, isn't new. Nor is it any great discovery. All you have to do is to walk outside on a cloudy day. The relative humidity might be higher, but chances are that the temperature will be lower.

The effects on Mars, however, caused many scientists to take closer notice of the possible effects of a long-lasting cloud of dust. The studies made concerning such clouds that resulted from various volcanic eruptions gave a positive indication that the situation on Mars wasn't unique. These studies showed that volcanic eruptions, and the resulting dust, smoke, and soot, have had worldwide effects on the climate of earth in the past.

The measurable and verifiable effects indicated shifts in the climate sufficient to cause problems. As deadly as some of these effects had been, what do they have to do with the theory that a nuclear war could cause the end of life on earth as we know it?

Changes of a degree or two have occurred, and the effects have been studied thoroughly. What would happen if the change in the climate was greater?

What was needed was a test case in which a more major climatic change seemed to be the result of a more major and longer-lasting cloud. What about the mass extinction that happened some 65 million years ago when more than 80 percent of all forms of life perished, including the dinosaurs?

Primordial Earth

In the beginning, our planet was very hot. Slowly the surface cooled enough to become solid. The planet and its atmosphere turned into a large chemical manufacturing plant. As the chemical reactions continued, water vapor developed along with those organic chemicals needed to produce life.

As the earth cooled, crust activity continued (and still does continue). Massive earthquakes and heavy volcanic activity changed both the surface of the planet and the atmosphere that surrounds it. Eventually the earth came to be covered with something else: life.

The most dramatic of these life forms was the dinosaur. Contrary to what many people think, most of the dinosaurs were rather small in size. A few were quite large. But large or small, for millions of years, the dinosaurs were the dominant animals on earth.

Scientists know quite a bit about the dinosaur era from the fossil remains. Often the information has to be pieced together, since relatively few whole fossils exist.

It takes a very special process for a living plant or creature to be turned into a fossil. If the creature dies and all conditions are normal, nature takes its recycling course and, within a very short time, little or nothing remains. Even when conditions are perfect for the for-

An artist's conception of dinosaurs
and other animals that inhabited
the earth in prehistoric times

mation of a fossil, other natural forces are at work that destroy them. After several millions of years, not much remains.

Dating of the fossils is done in several ways. The one most people are familiar with is carbon dating, which measures the amount of residual radiocarbon (carbon-14) in a carbon-combining object. Since carbon-14 decays at a known rate, the amount of radiocarbon is used to calculate the age of the object.

The second common method calculates the age of a fossil from the layer or depth at which it is found. (To oversimplify, if it takes 100,000 years for a layer to form, and there are 10 layers, something found in the tenth layer is somewhere around a million years old.) If the age of one object in a layer is known, other things found in that same layer are approximately the same age.

Using these and other methods, scientists know approximately when various things existed, and which things existed with which other things. (Movies showing a cave man fighting a dinosaur are nonsense, because the fossil record shows that the two never existed at the same time; in fact, they were millions of years apart.)

The Dinosaurs Disappear

The dinosaurs flourished for millions of years. And then, quite suddenly, about 65 million years ago, all the dinosaurs and about 80 percent of all other life forms ceased to exist. It is almost as though someone had drawn a very sharp line and said, "Before this, they exist. After this, they don't."

What could have happened to cause almost all life on the planet to blink out of existence so completely and in such a short period of time?

No one knows for sure just what happened, although there are a number of theories. Most of these have been dismissed by the scientific community. One theory suggests that a rogue star moved through—or at least near—our solar system, causing damage and massive changes. One of the more outlandish (or at least unscientific) theories says that aliens came to earth on a massive hunting trip.

Evidence seems to indicate that the magnetic polarity of earth shifts on an irregular basis. For a number of years, this and other planetary and solar shifts were thought to have been the cause of the worldwide extinction.

Although some scientists still hold with this theory, another theory is gaining popularity. It involves a sudden, global shift in the climate. Evidence seems to show that the shift was from warmer to colder temperatures.

But what might have caused this shift? One theory is that a large meteorite could have struck the earth. If the meteorite was large enough, its impact would have raised a cloud of dust that could stretch out and cover the earth, turning the entire planet as dark as Mount St. Helens made Yakima, Washington.

A Layer of Dust

If a meteor or comet had struck the earth with enough force to cause global extinction, some evidence of this should be available. Some have pointed to various sites that could have been caused by the collision. One example of this is the Bay of Biscay. Many others have been suggested, but to date no absolute proof has been found to indicate any specific site—or even to indicate that the earth was ever subjected to such a massive strike.

Then, in 1980, Walter and Louis Alvarez headed up a scientific team from the University of California at Berkeley. This group made the discovery that the earth has a layer of iridium-containing-clay 1 cm (about one half inch) thick, indicating that the layer was caused, at least in part, by a meteorite. This layer was found in rock formations that have been dated back 65 million years.

Below this layer are found the fossil remains of the dinosaurs and other species that existed with them, and of earlier creatures. Above it, they are all gone.

Some have said that this layer of clay could be positive proof of a disastrous collision of the earth with a huge meteor, comet, or other object. Others say that the layer is the result of a period in history when the earth happened to be heavily bombarded by numerous smaller meteorites.

Either way, a layer of meteoritic dust spread across the entire planet to that depth is a remarkable occurrence.

Brian Toon and the TTAPS group accepted this finding and set about trying to find out what would happen if the earth was covered with such a cloud of dust. To do this they took data obtained from the studies of volcanic eruptions, the results from the exploration of Mars, and all the information available on how the atmosphere of our planet functions. They then set up a computer model that would show the effects.

Brian Toon presented his findings at a meeting of scientists. The conclusion stated that such a dust cloud could easily cause a decrease in worldwide temperature to such an extent that very few forms of life would be able to survive. The decrease in temperature would immediately or eventually cause the death of a large portion of both the plants and animals. Without sunlight the plants could not photosynthesize. The remaining animals would starve to death from a lack of food, the plant eaters from a lack of plants, and then the carnivores from a lack of plant eaters.

There was general, although not unanimous, agreement with the validity of Toon's study. During the meeting, the question was raised concerning the effects of dust that would be thrown into the atmosphere as a result of a nuclear exchange.

New Studies Begin

Until 1975, all studies concerning the effects of a nuclear war of any size were based on the effects of single warhead blasts. These effects were well known and well documented. The amount of dust thrown into the atmosphere, and how high it would go, are reasonably well known. According to a 1975 report for the National Academy of Science (a group which is now a staunch supporter of the nuclear winter theory) for any single blast, this quantity is relatively insignificant, just as have been most volcanic eruptions. This report said that a nuclear war would have no appreciable effect on the climate.

What hadn't been taken into consideration was the combined effect of hundreds or thousands of nuclear detonations taking place within a very short period of time. Before the detailed studies of the effects of volcanic clouds on the climate were made, scientists had no accurate model on which to base their predictions.

In 1982 one of the first collections of articles concerning the long-term effects of nuclear war was published in a Swedish magazine called *Ambio*.

Dr. Paul Crutzen and Dr. John Birks studied the possibility of nuclear blasts producing ozone in the troposphere. This led them to make a study on the effects of smoke in the atmosphere from those blasts. This new study showed that forest fires alone caused by a nuclear war could produce sufficient smoke to block out the sun over significant portions of the planet.

Dr. Crutzen's study revealed that the equivalent of 100 million tons of smoke would be released into the atmosphere from forest fires alone. Other scientists say

that this is a low estimate, and that if a war occurs during the summer or during a dry period, the amount of smoke produced would be considerably higher. Adding to this cloud would be the smoke from burning cities. Bombing runs during World War II proved the possibility of firestorms. A major fire in Pittsburgh in 1974 showed that this situation could be much worse should a similar event occur again. The new synthetics and petrochemicals found in almost all modern cities burn easily, producing not only dense, black smoke, but also pyrotoxins (poisonous fumes released during burning).

The TTAPS Model

Using all of the available data, including that generated by Brian Toon, Richard Turco made a study of the primary targets of the world. Many of these were urban targets.

Tom Ackerman then developed a computer model to coordinate the information gathered and to help predict the effects. The 5,000-megaton baseline exchange, representing about a third of the warheads that existed in 1983, would throw approximately 1 billion tons of dust into the atmosphere. The model showed that up to 80 percent of this dust would reach the stratosphere. By itself, this would scatter 25 percent of the sunlight and reflect it back into space.

The TTAPS model also assumed that 5 percent of the explosions would cause firestorms, adding to the smoke blanket in the stratosphere. The rest of the smoke

The smoke from forest fires caused by a nuclear war could block out the sun over portions of the earth.

and dust brought about by the war would stay in the troposphere.

One computer model showed this thick layer of dust, smoke, and soot capable of absorbing, reflecting, and blocking up to 76 percent of the incoming sunlight. Almost all models that used as a starting point anything above 100 megatons showed a fairly quick reduction in light of down to 1 percent of normal, and a resultant temperature drop of as much as 144°F (80°C) below normal.

As a standard, the TTAPS model accepts a decrease to -9.4°F (-23°C) within a few days, and then a gradual increase in temperature back to the freezing point within about three months.

The National Center for Atmospheric Research in Colorado ran tests on the TTAPS model. By taking into account the temperature of the oceans and averaging this figure into the overall model, it predicted a global average temperature change about half that of the TTAPS model. Even so, it showed that by the eighth day after the battle much of the Northern Hemisphere would be below freezing even in mid-July. While this was a more optimistic viewpoint, the study also showed that the clouds could last much longer than originally predicted, because of massive temperature inversions.

Parallels

The amount of dust in the atmosphere 65 million years ago can be calculated by studying the thickness of the layer found by the Alvarez team. This quantity can then be combined with the known atmospheric effects, such as wind movement, rain, and other conditions. A computer model can then be generated, showing the overall effects of that dust cloud on the climate and on life.

The model thus generated shows a planet plunged into sudden darkness and temperatures far below freezing, both of which last for many months.

The TTAPS Model, predicting the results of a nuclear war, presents a very similar picture of earth. The computer models developed seem to indicate that the effects of a major nuclear war would be very much the same as what happened 65 million years ago. Some say that the effects would be worse since the fires and injections of dust and other particulates would take place over a wider range instead of just in one major spot. Other effects, unique to nuclear blasts, could also be present.

6

What Is Nuclear Winter?

On November 1, 1983, groups of international scientists gathered in both the United States and the Soviet Union. The two groups were linked by satellite. The topic of discussion was nuclear winter. The hope was that if enough scientists from enough countries participated, and attested to the validity of the studies, the various governments might take quicker notice—and quicker action.

The study most often used and quoted is the TTAPS study. It involves a series of computer scenarios, generated by "plugging in" known values and letting the computer come up with various predictions based on that knowledge. Some forty different scenarios were developed, each based on a different kind of attack, with varying amounts of force used.

Many other reports and studies have been made, such as the one by Vladamir Aleksandrov of the USSR. Of these, the vast majority concur with the general findings of the TTAPS study, and disagree only in a few minor details. Some have come to conclusions that the results would not necessarily be as severe as predicted by the TTAPS Model, but do show a global decrease in temperature of several degrees. They note, however, that "it is not necessary to envision a world dripping with ice before such disasters would occur."

The SCOPE-ENUWAR study of 1985 concludes, ". . . the indirect effects of a large-scale nuclear war could be more consequential globally than the direct effects."

There are three basic effects in a nuclear explosion: pressure, heat, and radiation. The pressure (force) of the explosion causes physical damage to anything that happens to be in the way. The heat burns anything in the way (including some things that don't normally burn). The radiation is more of a "side effect," but is still capable of killing, both during the explosion and later with the fallout.

Nuclear winter is more concerned with the first two.

According to a report published by the National Academy of Science in 1985, there would be 10 million metric tons of dust, and 25 million tons of smoke and soot lifted into the atmosphere for each megaton of explosive power. The more powerful the blast, the more smoke and dust there will be in the stratosphere.

All weather as we think of it takes place in the troposphere, the lower layer. The stratosphere is essentially stable in this regard. Consequently, anything that makes its way into the stratosphere tends to stay there. There is no rain to wash it out. The smaller the particle, the longer it will stay aloft.

A Nuclear Explosion—
The Beginning

In a single city, a 1-megaton warhead will first destroy by overpressure virtually all buildings within a 3-mile (5-kilometer) range. The heat will start fires at a distance of ten miles (16 kilometers) or more. As was demonstrated by both the nuclear bombings of Hiroshima and Nagasaki and the conventional bombings during World

War II, the smaller individual fires tend to combine to become a firestorm.

Tremendous quantities of dust, smoke, and soot enter the atmosphere. The city beneath will soon be hidden beneath a thick cloud. If this happens even to only a few cities, the clouds will eventually spread out and disperse.

For the purpose of the studies, it is assumed that a full-scale exchange will consist of at least 5,000 megatons. Many of these warheads will not be targeted for cities or even areas where a firestorm will result. Although neither superpower has a policy of specifically attacking civilian areas or cities, many of the military targets and secondary targets are in, or very near, large cities. With only 2,300 cities in the world, and more than 18,000 warheads, it is unlikely that very many cities would *not* be attacked.

Just as the individual fires on the ground combine, the clouds of dust spread out and combine in the atmosphere. In a matter of days the entire target zone of the Northern Hemisphere mid-latitudes is covered.

The upper part of the cloud will be reflecting and absorbing the sunlight that normally reaches the surface. This will create a temperature change, with the atmosphere of the Southern Hemisphere being much cooler. Within a few weeks the clouds begin to move south and across the equator, to eventually expand in a few months to cover a large portion of the planet.

Another temperature change will occur between the continental landmasses and the oceans. Oceans tend to be temperature-stable. It has been said that even if a severe nuclear winter lasts for over a year, the temperature of the oceans will not change very much.

Continental landmasses, however, will become much colder. Heavy winds, possibly lasting for weeks, will whip the coastal regions. This in turn causes several problems.

First, that wind is cold. Although the coastal regions will be considerably warmer than the inland areas, the winds will make things uncomfortable.

Second, the force of the winds could be strong enough to cause damage. It will at least cause some damage to the plants and crops.

Third, it will be extremely difficult, if not impossible, to take a boat or ship out onto the water. Fishing will have to stop.

Fourth, and perhaps most deadly of all, the winds could carry increased levels of radioactive fallout.

The Darkness and Cold

According to the TTAPS model, with a baseline of 5,000 megatons (one-third to one-half of the existing arsenals), within about ten days only 1 percent of the normal sunlight will be reaching the surface. (A worst-case study indicated that the amount of light could be reduced to as little as 0.1 percent of the normal average, while a test case of a limited nuclear war shows a decrease of 95 percent, down to 5 percent of normal.)

Depending on which model you choose, the darkness and the resulting decrease in temperature could last anywhere from a few weeks to years. The TTAPS model scenarios put the threshold attack of 100 megatons as causing the effect for about 3 months, while 10,000 megatons could produce a nuclear winter that would last for one year.

Attack	Percent Light after 1 week	Percent Light after 1 month	Duration of effect
100 MT	5 to 15%	15 to 40	3 months
5,000 MT	2 to 5%	5% to 35%	6 months
10,000 MT	less than 1%	less than 1%	1 year +

Very few plants can carry on photosynthesis with so little light. According to plant ecologist Joseph Berry, if the light level falls below 15 percent of normal, plants will not be able to grow. Many of the plants that survive the initial blasts, the fires, and the effects of radiation will still die for lack of sunlight.

Plants are not only a major part of the food chain, but are also at the base of the oxygen cycle. In the process of photosynthesis, carbon dioxide and water are converted into sugar. Oxygen is given off as a waste product. For this to happen, sunlight is needed. Take away the sun and photosynthesis stops. Levels of carbon dioxide build up while oxygen decreases. Although many groups do not see this as a serious threat, others say that it could create the final blow to oxygen-breathing life on earth.

Attack	Temperature after 1 week	Temperature after 1 month	Duration of effect
100 MT	0 to −10	−20 to −30	3 months
5000 MT	0 to −10	−30 to −40	up to 1 yr
10,000 MT	0 to −10	−40 to −50	1 year +

On land the plants also have to contend with a severe drop in temperature. According to the studies, the continents could suffer from temperatures of −20 C (−4 F), and remain there for weeks or months.

John Harte of the University of California has said that in a nuclear winter inland bodies of water would be covered by ice of up to 2 meters (about 6 feet) in thickness. With a lack of fuel for fires to melt the ice, death from thirst would result. Animals would certainly die from the combination of cold and the lack of food and water.

The oceans won't be affected nearly as much by the

cold, at least not for a long time. There is a very large quantity of water in the oceans, and water tends to resist change in temperature. Even as the land temperature drops far below freezing, the water in the ocean will remain at essentially the same temperature.

Some cite this as proof that nuclear winter won't cause the mass extinctions claimed. All the cattle might die, they say, but there is still all that life in the oceans which we can eat until everything returns to normal on land.

The problem with this idea is that the lack of sunlight will kill, or at least greatly decrease, plankton and other oceanic plants. Since these are the base of the food chain, as they disappear the food chain becomes disrupted. The fish and other animal life in the oceans might not feel the cold, but they will starve to death.

Even if there were plenty of fish, the heavy coastal winds will prevent us from getting them.

How Sensitive?

Agriculture has been studied for a very long time, in order to improve farming methods. Earlier studies have shown that a decrease of just 1 degree at a critical time can reduce crop production by as much as 10 percent.

An argument has been used that many plants on earth are tolerant of the cold, and in fact require periods of cold weather to grow and thrive. Yet, the plants must acclimatize slowly, as with the gradual change of seasons. Even cold-hardy plants will be killed or damaged if the temperature suddenly shifts from a warm 70° to below freezing.

In a speech sponsored by the Natural Resources Defense Council (NRDC), Carl Sagan said, "A single day below freezing is adequate to destroy the Japanese rice crop. An average temperature 3 degrees below normal is enough to destroy all wheat and barley in Canada."

The combination of cold and darkness would create a synergism—the two effects adding together to create an outcome that is greater than the sum of the two effects. For example, a plant damaged by sudden cold might survive if it has sufficient sunlight. The normal process of photosynthesis can greatly reduce the amount of permanent damage to the plant. Without the sunlight, a synergism takes place, with the cold and dark working together to cause more damage than the mere combination of damage of each.

Another synergism involves the function of bees. Many of the plants on earth rely on bees and other insects for pollination. Without pollination, the plants don't reproduce or grow. The combination of dark and cold will kill many of the insects outright. Others will survive, but won't do their job under those circumstances.

At the same time, many insects are relatively immune to the conditions that would result from a nuclear winter. Radiation affects them far less than it does higher life forms. Many species, if denied food and water, or if subjected to cold, will simply drop into an induced hibernation until conditions more to their liking return. The eggs of most insects are more resistant than are the adults, which means that although the majority of the adult insects are killed, many species are likely to survive even an extended nuclear winter.

Then, with fewer or no natural checks on their populations, the number of insects will increase dramatically. One study predicts insects as our prime competitor for food.

Birds, the major natural check on the insect population, are as sensitive to radioactivity as are humans. They are also very sensitive to cold and dark. With much of their food source either destroyed or temporarily in hibernation, many of the birds that survive a nuclear war will die of starvation and cold.

Another Effect

After the clouds clear away, the earth will be given yet another dose of radiation, this time from the sun. Because of depletion of the ozone, increased levels of ultraviolet-B will reach the surface, causing further sterilization, mutation, and disease. There is no way to accurately predict how long this would continue, but the indications are that, despite the self-repairing nature of the ozone layer, it would not recover completely until about two years later.

Using the 5,000-megaton baseline, the TTAPS model predicts a reduction of up to about 30 percent of the ozone, which would in effect double the amount of ultraviolet-B striking the surface of the earth. A 10,000-megaton war could double the depletion, thus causing even more irradiation.

A Soviet study says that the increase in solar radiation could actually cause a "nuclear summer," with temperatures ranging from 77° to 95°F (25° to 35°C) above normal, following the nuclear winter. Many scientists disagree with this theory, but admit that the possibility exists.

How Long? How Bad?

There is some evidence, although none conclusive, that the nuclear winter could last for years rather than months. Other studies indicate that the worst will be over in a matter of weeks.

*A Japanese family walks to the
village temple through rice paddies.
The Japanese rice crop could be
destroyed by one freezing day of
"nuclear winter."*

The problem is that no one knows for sure. Short of actually having a nuclear war, whether or not nuclear winter can occur cannot be proved. Nor is it possible to absolutely predict how bad a nuclear winter would be if it did occur. It could be less severe than the present computer model predictions—or it could be worse.

A computer-generated map of the world, using the baseline case (5,000 MT) shows that the temperature *could* drop as much as 144°F (80°C) in mid-July within twenty days after the war. One study, now dismissed by almost all scientists, says that the temperature will drop low enough, and stay that way long enough, to cause the oceans to freeze. Other studies indicate a drop in temperature of only a few degrees as a global average.

The threshold in the TTAPS model—the amount of nuclear explosive power if used on cities alone—is a mere 100 megatons. As you can see from the two charts on pages 58 and 59, the differences between such an attack and a more general attack of 5,000 megatons are minor, and are mostly in the amount of time the "winter" lasts.

Human recovery cannot go faster than the recovery of natural systems. If a nuclear winter lasts only three months but destroys worldwide harvests for two years, it will be two years before recovery can begin. Any species that are made extinct will obviously never recover, and if an extinct species is a crucial part of the food chain, the rest of that chain will fall apart in a domino effect.

If, for example, the darkness destroys *all* of the photoplankton in the ocean—that is, makes plankton extinct—then any creature dependent on plankton will either have to find some other suitable substitute, or will follow the plankton into extinction. Anything dependent on *that* creature will face the same situation, and so on up the chain.

7

The New Scenario

The immediate results of a nuclear war are well known. The explosive power, heat, and radioactivity are known quantities. The number of deaths for any given single warhead and under a number of different circumstances can also be predicted.

New tests are being performed either to further verify or to refute the claims of the nuclear winter theory. For example, the Royal Society of Canada has conducted a special study, titled "Nuclear Winter and Associated Effects." As a test case, 2.5 square miles (6.5 square kilometers) of forest was set afire using a substance similar to napalm. This section of forest, mostly balsam fir, had been killed by an infestation of budworm during the 1960s.

The purpose of the study was to observe and measure the convection columns from the fire. Dr. Andrew Forester and Richard Turco hope to use the results as a small representation of what could happen in a major nuclear exchange.

The findings of this test, and other studies, are still being compiled. As the work goes on, the new indications have caused scientists to revise the estimates of damage brought on by even the known effects.

Radiation

On March 1, 1954, the United States exploded a test 15-megaton device over the Bikini Atoll. Hydrogen bombs were new at this time, and the results weren't always accurate. In this case, the power was almost double what was predicted. Also unpredicted was the overall effect of the fallout. It swept across the Marshall Islands (specifically, Rongelap) 125 miles (200 kilometers) from the test site. Despite almost instant medical assistance, many of the people, and most of the children, began to develop many long-term medical problems as a result of the fallout.

Original studies of single-warhead blasts took radioactive fallout into account: fallout, immediately after the explosion, concentrated in and downwind from the target area; and long-term fallout as it drifts back out of the upper atmospheric layers a year or more later.

Of prime concern had been the immediate radioactive dose received. Early tests showed that even with adequate medical care, half of all adults exposed to 350 to 400 rads over a 48-hour period would die. The death rate among the elderly and the very young would be even higher. It was also shown that a dose of about 100 rads could cause serious problems, made even more serious if medical aid is not close at hand.

To give you an idea of how much radiation this is, a single medical X ray gives you a dose of about one-tenth of a rad. A 400-rad dose would be like getting about 4,000 X rays all at once.

According to some findings, a severe 10,000-megaton war could provide radiation exposure of more than 500 rads over approximately 30 percent of the area of the Northern Hemisphere, with the highest concentrations near the heaviest centers of population.

The long-term fallout wasn't as critical. It has been assumed, probably justifiably, that much of the radioactive dust and debris would be lifted into the stratosphere, where it would remain for a long period of time. By the time this dust found its way back to earth, most of the radioactivity would have disappeared, and the dose received would be relatively small.

New studies are now taking into account medium-term fallout. This is the dust and debris that falls back to earth within the first month or so after detonation.

Assuming that the winds and normal propagation of the atmosphere cause a more or less even distribution, the average dose would be somewhere around twenty rads in the entire Northern Hemisphere, but would be more like fifty rads through the middle latitudes, with twice this dose possible in certain areas. Just as people would be contaminated, so would food supplies, possibly adding as much as another fifty rads to the overall dose.

Fires

The World War II bombing of cities such as Dresden showed that fires can start and grow, then combine to create a firestorm. As surface temperature in the area quickly increases hundreds of degrees, people are killed by the incredible heat and by asphyxiation.

In a firestorm, the temperature of the surroundings would be somewhere around 1,472°F (800°C), or about four times as hot as a *hot* oven. In Dresden and Hamburg the only survivors were those who fled their shelters.

Modern cities will burn even more dangerously. Synthetic materials can burn hotter and produce poisonous fumes. The smoke produced by the fires would be denser than the fires of World War II. The difference has been described by comparing a wood fireplace to a burning automobile tire. According to the new studies, the smoke will not only kill people in the immediate

vicinity of the fire but will also spread into the atmosphere and, along with the dust, block out the sunlight.

Some estimates claim that as much as 25 million tons of smoke and soot could be produced per megaton of explosive over a city. Added to the sizable amount of dust thrown aloft, the predicted effect, according to computer models would be a lessening of sunlight.

TTAPS

The TTAPS group studied and analyzed about 40 different scenarios, ranging from a 100-megaton exchange (1,000 warheads) to a more severe exchange of 10,000 megatons. Based on the number of likely targets in the world, they used a 5,000 megaton exchange as an "average" nuclear war. This was called the "baseline exchange." They also concentrated attention on the effects of a preemptive first strike of 3,000 megatons, with no retaliation.

The kind of attack determines the effects. An airburst, for example, tends to destroy large areas of the surface, while a ground burst—such as would be used to knock out missile silos—would tend to throw more dust into the atmosphere.

It is difficult to determine just how much dust would reach the atmosphere and particularly the stratosphere (where the particles would remain for a longer period of time). Actual nuclear tests indicate that there would be somewhere between 100,000 and 600,000 tons of dust per megaton of explosive. The TTAPS study assumed

In World War II, firestorms as well as bombs were responsible for the devastation of the beautiful city of Dresden, Germany.

330,000 tons per megaton for surface bursts, and 100,000 tons per megaton for near-surface bursts.

The baseline study of 5,000 megatons was calculated on the basis that 57 percent of all explosions (5,928 detonations out of a total of 10,400) would be surface bursts. The 3,000-megaton preemptive strike was based on 50 percent (1,125 of 2,250) being surface bursts. A severe 10,000-megaton exchange assumed that 63 percent (10,181 of 16,160) would be surface bursts.

Predicting the amount of smoke and soot is even more difficult. There are many factors involved, such as the site of the detonation, the time of year, the weather, and so forth. For example, a 1-megaton airburst over a major modern city will cause considerably more smoke, soot, and pyrotoxins than will the same explosion over a missile base on the desert. In rainy weather, or during the winter, the extent of forest and other ground fires will be greatly reduced.

It is primarily this uncertainty that causes many people to think of nuclear winter as being less probable than supposed by the TTAPS study. However, the TTAPS model supporters claim that the 100-megaton exchange scenario on cities produces the same results as the 5,000-megaton baseline. If the model shows that a 100-megaton battle—a relatively minor one—could produce a nuclear winter, then a larger war would also do so, regardless of the season or targets.

A Soviet Viewpoint

Yuri Izrael of the Soviet Union said that, in a study done in the USSR, indications were that after a few weeks only about 1 percent of the dust and soot would remain. He said that while this would still create cold on the surface sufficient to be devastating, it might not be as severe, or as long-lasting, as suggested by the TTAPS model.

He then said that the Soviet study showed instead that along with greatly increased levels of ultraviolet-B there would be increased levels of "gaseous admixtures" in the atmosphere and a doubling of carbon dioxide. This, in turn, would cause a greenhouse effect on earth, causing the average temperature to go up considerably.

Whatever differences there were in the method, Izrael's conclusion was the same: "In the final analysis, all sides suffer fatally."

Another Soviet scientist, Dr. Kontratyev, mentioned previous studies done concerning nuclear tests from 1961 and 1962. These tests showed that another by-product of a nuclear blast is a high level of nitrogen dioxide. All by itself, he said, this could cause a world-wide decrease in temperature of up to 18°F (10°C) and would last much longer than any dust trapped in the atmosphere.

Sergei Kapitza, in the October 1985 issue of the Bulletin of Atomic Scientists, said, "In the case of nuclear winter, this concept has come to stay with us. We cannot disinvent it, even if future research clarifies some details and imposes certain limits."

Food Shortages

After the winter begins to disappear, and as the surface weather returns to something like normal, there are other problems to face. Those few still left alive will emerge to a destroyed civilization. Problems of food shortage will continue for some time. There is a slight possibility that the food chain will never quite recover, and it certainly won't be as we know it.

A change of just a few degrees can be devastating to crops. According to agriculture specialist David Pimentel, the combined effect of cold and lack of sunlight could destroy "at least one year's harvest, and possibly two."

Under the best of conditions, a large city contains in it enough food and supplies to last the populace a week or less. This is a rough average. In some areas, the amount of food and other supplies would last longer; in others it would be less.

For a family of four to survive healthily for one year they would need 60 dozen eggs, 220 pounds (99 kilograms) of fruit, 370 pounds (167 kilograms) of vegetables, 540 pounds (243 kilograms) of potatoes, 200 loaves of bread, 820 pints (385 liters) of milk, and 520 pounds (234 kilograms) of meat. In addition, the average American family today uses between 73,000 to 219,000 gallons (277,000 to 832,000 liters) of water per year.

The only food presently stored in quantity is grain. For the most part this grain is kept in places that would be inaccessible to the majority of survivors. Chances are that it would be contaminated with radioactivity.

There would also be very few animals left alive to produce eggs, milk, or meat. Those that did survive would be our direct competitors for other food, such as grain.

In discussing the effects of the lack of fuel to run farm equipment after such a war, Dr. Pimentel said that with machinery it presently takes approximately ten hours to farm a hectare (four hours for an acre). If all tillage, cultivating, and harvesting had to be done by hand without the use of powered equipment, the same crop would require 1,200 hours per hectare (486 hours per acre).

He said, "We could not produce our crops with manpower alone, even if you got everybody in the United States working on the farm."

Obviously, with the proper conditions the survivors could cultivate some crops, but not enough to produce a balanced diet. They could, that is, if conditions are proper, and if they could find uncontaminated soil with sufficient water.

*Even if there were farms to cultivate after
a nuclear war, the lack of fuel would make
essential farm machinery inoperable.*

The effects of the food shortage would first be felt in the cities, where crops cannot be raised. It would then reach out and affect the rest of the world, including those parts that were not otherwise afflicted.

America exports about half of the world's total tonnage of grain. The Northern Hemisphere as a whole is sometimes called "the world's breadbasket." Without food grown in America or in the Northern Hemisphere, many more people in the world would starve than do now.

Movement across the Equator

It is assumed that the vast majority of the detonations would occur in the Northern Hemisphere. The initial effects of nuclear winter would begin, and would be more severe, north of the equator. Some scientists say that the normal wind flow at the equator will keep it that way. Others disagree.

Normally the winds from the north that reach the equator are deflected back to the north again as they come up against the southern winds. Under normal conditions, it takes a very long time for the atmosphere of the Northern Hemisphere to mix with that of the Southern Hemisphere.

After a major nuclear war, the cloud of dust and smoke will cause the temperature on the surface to drop by absorbing and reflecting sunlight. As it does this, and as demonstrated within the Martian atmosphere, the upper atmosphere gets hotter.

However, without its own cloud of dust, the atmosphere in the Southern Hemisphere would stay relatively cool. Scientists say that this would cause a natural movement of air from the hotter northern regions into the cooler southern atmosphere.

Stanley Thompson of the Colorado-based National Center for Atmospheric Research says that dense streamers of smoke, soot, and dust could drift to the Southern Hemisphere within a few days and would drop the surface temperature below freezing. If this prediction is accurate, nuclear winter will spread out to cover almost the entire globe. Some studies indicate that the surface temperature will rise after the winter subsides, possibly to as high as 63°F (35°C) above normal.

Other Aftereffects

The heat and energy of a nuclear blast is sufficient to cause the nitrogen of the atmosphere to burn, turning it into various oxides of nitrogen. The nitrogen oxides have the effect of destroying the ozone layer.

According to the latest findings, the amount of ultraviolet-B radiation striking the earth could at least double. Those who have survived through all the rest will be then subjected to this dangerous radiation.

Proneness to disease will have increased from a variety of causes. Sanitation will have collapsed along with everything else. There will also be several billion corpses as yet unburied—but very few around to do the job. The increased ultraviolet-B will make matters worse by causing higher rates of skin cancer and other problems. Many plants and animals will also be affected by the more dangerous sunlight.

If the theory of nuclear winter is correct, many different species of plant and animal will become extinct. And as one species "goes," it takes with it any other species that is dependent on it for survival.

According to Paul Ehrlich, "If there is a full-scale nuclear war, odds are you can kiss the Northern Hemisphere goodbye. . . . Odds are also that the effects will be catastrophic in the Southern Hemisphere." He went on to say that if the TTAPS model is any indication, you "could not preclude the extinction of Homo sapiens."

In a pamphlet titled, "To Preserve a World Graced by Life," Carl Sagan wrote, "The dangers of nuclear war are, in a way, well-known. But in a way they are not well-known, because of the psychological factor—psychiatrists call it denial—that makes us feel it's so horrible that we might as well not think about it. This element of denial is, I believe, one of the most serious problems we face."

Professor Richard Lifton of John Jay College in New York believes that the decrease of importance of the family as a unit is one result of the constant fear of nuclear war. He believes that many Americans have "a sense of radical futurelessness."

Dr. John Mack of Harvard echoes this sentiment, saying that fears of worldwide annihilation have brought on feelings of cynicism, sadness, bitterness, and a sense of helplessness. Others have even said that the fear of nuclear war has led to such ills as the increasing lack of morality, the decreasing quality of American-made products, and the higher sense of materialism—"Get it while you can because it might not be here tomorrow."

$$\begin{array}{c} \boxed{\begin{array}{c} 0 \\ 0 \end{array}} \end{array}$$

What Are the Alternatives?

At the beginning of our "Nuclear Age," many scientists involved with the research banded together in an effort to convince the American government to consider seriously the consequences of the use of atomic energy. Bertrand Russell was the author of a short piece, which was then signed by other scientists, Einstein among them. It came to be known as the Russell-Einstein Manifesto. It reads like this:

> *We have to learn to think in a new way. Remember your humanity and forget the rest. If you can do so, the way lies open to a new paradise; if you cannot, there lies before you the risk of universal death.*

This was written long before the concept of nuclear winter was developed and researched. The scientists involved were thinking more along the lines of the immediate destruction of cities and lives due to the power of a nuclear explosion. As yet they hadn't foreseen the possibility of a nuclear winter, or the possibility of "universal death," that is, the destruction of every living thing on earth.

Even so, the predicted deaths of at least half of all

people on earth is frightening. From even the single-warhead studies, it was shown that 75 percent of people in America and in Russia could lose their lives either immediately from the direct effects of the explosions, or later from the radiation poisoning, injuries, lack of care and food, disease, and so forth.

In a recent talk, Dr. Carl Sagan said that just one of our modern strategic submarines can destroy between 150 and 192 cities in the Soviet Union. His point was that if this wasn't sufficient to deter outrageous acts on the part of the Soviet Union, what would be? "Two submarines? Three? But three submarines can destroy more cities than there *are* in the Soviet Union."

Disarmament?

The ideal alternative to a nuclear holocaust is total peace on earth among all nations. Almost as idealistic is disarmament, at least to the point where nuclear winter cannot happen. Some people, having realized that total disarmament is improbable, have suggested that we at least reduce the number of warheads to below the point where nuclear winter could occur. This would be a reduction by at least 90 percent, leaving each side only 10 percent of what exists and allowing new weapons to be built only to replace those that become obsolete. Carl Sagan, one of the authors of the first reports on nuclear winter, has said that such extreme arms reductions are necessary "for the same reasons that were used to justify the arms race in the first place."

But is disarmament, or even a reduction in arms, a

*The nuclear-powered fleet
ballistic missile submarine
USS James Madison at sea*

likely solution? Most say that it isn't. The level of distrust, and even hatred, between the two superpowers is such that neither is ready to take even the slightest chance of leaving the other with an advantage over them. To date, instead of decreasing the number of weapons (let alone agreeing to total disarmament), both superpowers have continued to add to the stockpile of weapons and warheads.

Addressing the 1981 Harvard commencement, Thomas J. Watson Jr., former U.S. ambassador to the Soviet Union, said, "Between us, our two countries now have explosive power equal to a million Hiroshima A-bombs. We have between us some 15 thousand 'city killing' weapons—one bomb, one city. Bigger stockpiles do not mean more security. Enough is enough. And we are far beyond that point now."

Thomas D. Cabot echoed this sentiment in an article published in the July-August 1984 issue of *Harvard Magazine*. "The nuclear-weapons argument sounds like boys soaked in gasoline arguing about who has the most matches."

During the 1980s, an additional 5,000 warheads were added to the stockpile. Plans have been made to nearly double the total before the end of the century.

Nuclear Freeze?

One way to deter nuclear holocaust is to put a halt to the arms race. All the nations of the world, particularly those with existing nuclear weapons, would have to agree to cease building new ones.

Few people see a nuclear freeze as a viable end to the threat of global destruction. After all, if no new weapons are introduced into the stockpiles, there are still in existence many times more than enough to trigger nuclear winter. It would not change the fact that there now exist enough weapons to destroy all life even without a nuclear winter.

However, some experts see a nuclear freeze as a good first step. Once we have agreed to stop the arms race, it should be easier to come up with a viable solution to further disarmament.

Dr. Edward Teller, called "the father of the hydrogen bomb," has said of a nuclear freeze, "It has been claimed to be as simple as a can opener. It is also as useful in preventing nuclear war as a can opener."

Dr. Carl Sagan has said, "The danger is so large, and the nuclear arsenals grow every day, that merely being content with it not getting worse is insufficient."

Some have suggested an immediate decrease in weapons of perhaps 5 percent or 10 percent across the board. The idea is that, while such a minor arms reduction would be almost useless, both in preventing worldwide destruction and in preventing a nuclear winter, it is a starting point. Proponents of this idea say that the reduction is small enough so that verifiability won't matter quite so much, which in turn makes the agreement easier to negotiate.

Arms Negotiations

Speaking of the need to come up with a solution and agreement of some sort, Thomas J. Watson, Jr. said, "Against all these illusions, what is the reality? The reality is that thermonuclear war in any form is suicide. Above all, the time has come for a new effort to cap the strategic arms race—cap it through a verifiable treaty which gives both sides the security they require."

Negotiations have been, and will continue to be, difficult. Neither of the two superpowers trusts the other. And although both sides now admit to the possibility, if not probability, of nuclear winter, neither feels that it can afford to allow the other side even the slightest advantage.

As long as this philosophy continues, any treaties are likely to be limited in scope. Until the negotiators "learn to think a new way," as Einstein said, most experts feel that disarmament will be an unrealized dream.

Thomas D. Cabot wrote, "It is not sympathy for or empathy with the Russians that we need, it is a clear understanding of why they feel threatened and are impelled to build more armaments. We will not succeed in negotiations by increasing their fears nor they by increasing ours."

The late Senator Henry Jackson and former Ambassador Watson suggested that the respective governments set up a Soviet-American Joint Consultation Center. The center would be staffed by important personnel from both sides. Whenever an incident occurred in the world (such as the Korean airliner being shot down in 1983, or the United States firing on Libya in 1986), both sides would get into immediate contact to discuss things before they could get out of hand. The two sides would then report to their respective governments.

According to Jackson and Watson, the two potential enemies wouldn't have to rely strictly on the "hot line" but would have a face-to-face encounter in times of crisis. Further, the constant daily contact between the staffs during noncritical times could help to prevent outbursts of anger and would increase credibility when one side or the other makes certain claims.

Watson was quoted as saying that one of the largest values of such a center would be "to keep the pressure down from where either one of us might do something senseless."

Star Wars"

On March 23, 1983, President Ronald Reagan announced a new plan for national defense called "Strategic Defense Initiative," or SDI. It was quickly nicknamed "Star Wars." The plan called for weapons of defense to be placed in space around the earth.

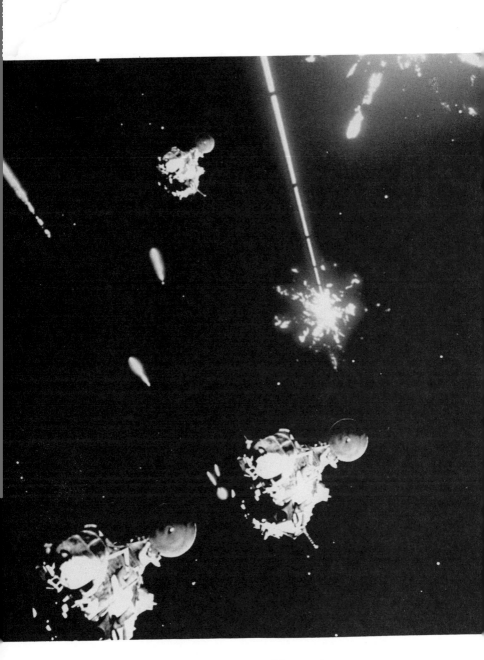

A fictional conception of Strategic Defense Initiative, or "Star Wars"

The idea of SDI is to develop a system that could intercept and destroy incoming missiles before they could reach their targets or cause other damage. If such a system could work, our country would be virtually invulnerable to attack.

The plan, as promoted by General Daniel Graham, and named "High Frontier," calls for a three-part system. The first part would be to place 432 satellites in orbit around the earth. These would be armed with non-nuclear missiles and high-power chemical lasers. The primary function of this first layer of defense would be to shoot down missiles immediately after launch or while in the early parts of their trajectories.

Behind this would be more non-nuclear missiles, primarily ground-based, that would intercept more of the incoming weapons. The main purpose of this defense layer would be to protect the missile sites. (According to the plan, the system would not be expanded to protect cities until sometime in the next century, if then.)

A third layer would consist of "particle beam weapons and other Star Wars defenses." The technology for this third layer does not exist at this time.

The plan was submitted to the Pentagon. On November 24, 1982, Secretary of Defense Caspar Weinberger sent a response to General Graham that indicated he was unwilling to commit to a system for which all needed technology did not exist. He has since changed his public viewpoint of the system.

The Office of Technology Assessment did a further study of the system, and described it as "a defensive system of extremely limited capability," and then went on to say that if the Soviets upgraded their present offensive missiles, the system would then have "no capability."

Paul Nitze, a prominent governmental advisor, brought up two points to consider. First, an effective defense system must not itself be vulnerable to attack. If the enemy can easily knock out that system it "would decrease, rather than enhance, stability."

Second, it must be less expensive to build the defense than it is to build the offense. If the system costs $100 billion to build, and the enemy can build enough offensive weapons to reach the capacity of that system for $10 billion, it becomes economically unfeasible. For each $100 billion we spend on the system, it would cost the enemy just one-tenth to render the system useless.

But that "if" is a large one indeed. It's not difficult to find critics of the system. Most say that instead of bringing the arms race to a halt, it will accelerate that race.

George Ball, former deputy secretary of state and U.S. ambassador to the United Nations, said of SDI, "The Soviets would never sit idly by watching us struggle to build a shield behind which—as they saw it—we might safely launch a first strike." Some critics claim this means that if the Soviets believe that SDI would work, they would take that ridiculous gamble and start an all-out war before SDI could be put into effect, a possibility increased by the official United States policy of possibly using a preemptive first strike. Others say that whether the system works or not, it will cause the Soviets to build even more offensive missiles, along with thousands of "decoys," thus overtaxing the system while spending very little. Many say that, at the very least, it will further push the Soviets into a LOW (launch-on-warning) stance, thus increasing the danger of an accidental nuclear war.

Optimistic reactions are that such a system could stop as many as 95 percent of incoming missiles, if the number of missiles remains at the present level, but some experts say that the system will do well to stop just half of the incoming warheads. Increase the number of incoming missiles, and more will get through. The TTAPS group points out that as little as 2 percent of what now exists might trigger a nuclear winter, and emphasizes that the arms race is, if anything, increasing. And many experts say that SDI will put "new life" into the arms race, accelerating it far beyond what we've already seen.

Prevention?

Another alternative to nuclear winter is to develop a means to prevent it from happening, but without giving up our weaponry.

For example, one of the primary contributions to the cause of nuclear winter would be the tremendous amounts of smoke and soot thrown into the atmosphere. Prevent this from happening and you just might prevent, or at least lessen, the effects of a nuclear attack. Several methods of doing this have been suggested.

One method is to maintain control of the conflict until such time as less would burn. During the winter, or during a rainy season, firestorms are less likely to spread. There is also a decreased (or nonexistent) chance that all the forests, crops, and fields will burn. Those who disagree say that, due to the tremendous heat involved, virtually anything close to the blast will ignite, regardless of how wet or cold it is. A lot of smoke and soot will be released into the atmosphere regardless of the time of year or conditions.

That further effects can be reduced by careful targeting is another suggestion. This can be done in two ways.

First, attacks on nonmilitary targets can be limited. This would mean that fewer cities would burn, and the air wouldn't be quite so filled with smoke, soot, and released pyrotoxins.

The problem with this solution, according to the scientists who are studying nuclear winter, is that even in the "off season" it could take as little as 100 megatons to start a nuclear winter. They also say that even though cities and civilian targets are not specifically attacked as such, many critical military targets happen to be in or near large cities.

If a nuclear winter occurred during a normal winter, the effects of increased cold wouldn't be nearly the problem it would be during the other seasons. After all, the argument goes, the plants and crops are already in hibernation.

Opposed to this is the theory that while the heaviest damage to the environment would result from warm weather turning cold, the additional freeze even during winter would both overfreeze existing plants and cause the "winter" to extend beyond its normal season, thus still causing massive damage to the environment. Also, the effects of a nuclear winter could last up to, and possibly more than, one year. If this happened, the freeze would still continue beyond the capability of the plants to recover.

Second, airburst and even ground-burst attacks can be limited. Instead, a tactic used during World War II could be used. The "blockbuster" bomb of World War II didn't explode until it had crashed through the buildings and the ground. A nuclear weapon could be designed to penetrate the ground (including concrete) and detonate only after it was beneath the target. The result would be a nearly equally destructive explosion, with the buildings above falling into the crater made by the warhead, but there would be greatly lessened heat, radiation, and fallout.

Opponents claim that while this can reduce the firestorms, the depth required to keep fires below the nuclear winter threshold is far too great. Warheads may not be able to penetrate to any appreciable depth in an attack on a city.

They also point once more to the findings of the TTAPS studies, showing that as little as 100 megatons can set off a nuclear winter, and claim that in a major exchange, at least this much equivalent force will affect the surface. Of the primary targets of a nuclear exchange, the missile silos and military targets will be among the first hit. For an effective strike, an under-

Minuteman missiles in underground silos,
like this one in South Dakota, would be
primary targets in nuclear war.

ground explosion simply will not do an effective job. Consequently, they claim, if the military does not accept this kind of attack, they will merely double or triple the number of warheads detonated at a particular target, and end up creating the same effect as if this kind of assault had never been considered.

Another solution suggested involves an after-war attack on those particles that get tossed into the atmosphere. The quantity, size, and altitude can be predicted from the studies. Consequently, it can also be determined how much force is needed to burn away, and thus destroy and dissipate, those particles.

New studies undertaken by meteorologists indicate that the energy needed to burn away the particles would be equal to, or less than, the energy needed to cast them aloft. Even if the atmosphere is filled to sun-blocking capacity, those particles can be burned away to nothingness, either by ground-based lasers or more likely by nuclear warheads detonated high in the atmosphere, thus ending any onset of nuclear winter.

Once again the opposition has objections. First, even though both sides have hundreds of warheads set aside for "after the war," it's possible, and even likely, that neither will have the capability to launch those warheads. The idea of a major exchange, they say, is to prevent that possibility, not to allow the enemy to have any remaining missiles or silos.

Second, and perhaps more important, if there are a billion tons of dust in the atmosphere, those billion tons have to go somewhere. If you burn a ton of paper on the ground, you end up with some relatively lightweight ash, but this is because much of the original weight has gone into the atmosphere. The original ton still exists somewhere. Since the earth is essentially a "closed system," the original mass will still remain on earth.

According to this objection, those countless particles trapped in the atmosphere will merely be turned into countless smaller particles which will do nothing more than go higher and remain longer, with the added detriment that they will have an even higher level of radioactivity. This solution, it is said, won't solve the problem—it will just make it worse and longer lasting.

A third objection is that the explosion of a nuclear weapon in the atmosphere would further deplete the precious ozone layer. Even if it could decrease the cloud, and thus warm the surface and help to prevent such a severe "winter," the end result would be an even higher increase in the amounts of ultraviolet-B radiation.

9

A Summary: Worlds of the Future

Assume for a moment that a major exchange has taken place. You were far enough away from any of the blasts and you've survived that initial assault.

Your next task will be to survive the aftereffects. Depending on how close you were to the blast, you may be suffering from burns or other physical injuries. Getting professional medical help will be next to impossible. The attempt alone probably means that you (and millions of others) will have to find your way to whatever medical facilities still exist. It probably also means that you'll have to move closer to a city, and face the possible danger of increased radiation.

All around you will be many people who were less fortunate than you were. They survived the blast, but their burns and injuries are more severe. Many are also suffering the obvious symptoms of radiation sickness. The streets are full of the dead, and the near dead. Most of those who do manage to get medical help will die.

According to FEMA studies, in the entire country there are just 62,000 intensive care beds and only 1,300 "burn" beds. Statistics indicate that a major nuclear war will leave, at the most, only about a third of the existing medical facilities and personnel. If the survival rate is as

expected, each surviving physician will be treating at least 1,700 patients in desperate need of medical attention. If the doctor gives each just ten minutes, and works constant twelve-hour days, it would take about twenty-four days to see each victim once. But it's unrealistic to think that ten minutes will be enough to treat many of the injuries, or that repeat treatments won't be needed immediately.

A typical American city has in it enough food to last for one week. If the city was a target, much of that will have been destroyed. Of what remains, most will be contaminated and its use will add to the already high radiation dose received. Radiation sickness increases, affecting more than half of all healthy adults and killing most of the young and the elderly.

With power gone, along with most other services, the only available water will be what can be removed from the lines and pipes, and it, too, might be contaminated with radioactivity. Sanitation will be a shambles. The streets will be littered with the dead, with no one there to handle burial. Most of the things we take for granted—a toilet that flushes, an electric light, the corner grocery store—will be gone.

Along with all other services, transportation of goods will be all but nonexistent. There might be millions of tons of uncontaminated grain stored in silos in Kansas, but it will do the people of New York City or Los Angeles no good. The truck drivers and train engineers will have more important things to do than to try to make runs into contaminated and dangerous areas either without

Nuclear protesters lie on the steps of the Belgian Bourse (stock exchange). A mock nuclear missile sticks out of a step.

pay, or for money that no longer has any value. Even if they were willing, there's no fuel to operate the vehicles.

Later the epidemics set in. Lack of food, medical care, and sanitation change what would have been no more than a relatively minor outbreak into something devastating. Millions more die.

If there are surrounding cities that have not been hit, there might be more assistance available, but chances are that those other cities will be in a similar situation. If they are not, it's unlikely that people there will want to give their precious supplies away.

Recovery would be slow, if at all possible. Radioactive contamination could last for years. As tests on the Bikini Atoll showed, devastation reaches out for some distance beyond the actual blast area. In this case the inhabitants on some of the Marshall Islands some distance away were contaminated and required medical care. Bikini itself became uninhabitable. Great efforts were made to make the islands habitable again, including removing and replacing several inches of the topsoil. In 1967 the inhabitants returned to the island, but in a short time it was determined that the level of radioactivity was still dangerously high, and once again the people had to move away. It wasn't until 1980, after even more extensive decontamination efforts, that the islands were once again declared to be safe. Even so, half of the food has to be imported.

But, after a war there will be no crews to reclaim and decontaminate the land, nor any place from which to import even 1 percent of the needed food.

These are the projected results of a major nuclear war, as studied and noted *before* the introduction of the nuclear-winter theories.

The Pessimistic View

The initial attacks have caused massive firestorms. Many of those who managed to find shelter from the immediate effects of the explosions are incinerated or are asphyxiated within those shelters. The immediate temperature on the ground is in the thousands of degrees. Later, as the firestorms spread, it's still far hotter than the hottest standard oven. The fires consume the oxygen. Huge clouds of poisonous gas blanket the city.

Within a couple of days, the cold begins to set in. The sun is all blotted out. Even those areas that were far from the blasts are affected. The plants begin to freeze and die. You almost wish that the cities and forests were still burning, just for some warmth. It has already dropped below the freezing point and continues to get colder until it is more than $-100°F$ ($-73°C$), despite the fact that it's mid-July.

As the plants die, the few remaining animals die. But it wouldn't be safe to eat those animals (or the plants, for that matter) since they are probably contaminated with the radioactive fallout that continues to rain down on the land like hot snow.

Still more millions die, both from the cold and from starvation. There is no decay yet—although you know that will come eventually—since the corpses are frozen solid.

You've heard rumors of some isolated groups of survivors who have turned to cannibalism. There's no way to verify this, since there are no communications.

Those conditions persist for months. You're almost alone now. Very few others have survived with you. Most of those are very sick, and you yourself always feel ill.

Slowly the skies begin to clear. About nine months after the holocaust you even get an occasional glimpse of the sun.

The land is totally barren. Even the skeletons of dead trees are gone, long ago burned for warmth. Still, the sun *is* coming back, and the earth *is* slowly warming again. Soon you can take those hoarded packages of seeds and attempt to plant them.

But you'd better be careful when you are outside. Chemical reactions in the stratosphere have depleted the ozone layer. Ultraviolet-B is pouring down, almost literally sterilizing the surface of the earth, and causing even more cancer in any animals or humans that have managed to survive.

Even as your precious crops start to sprout, they are destroyed by insects. Birds are killed more quickly by radiation than are insects. Consequently, more birds will be affected by nuclear war than will members of the insect family. The end result is a plague of insects, eating what few crops and plants remain.

The plagues aren't restricted to insects, however. There is the lack of sanitation, the billions of thawing corpses with no one to bury them all, the almost total lack of medical care, and the increased susceptibility to disease from the effects of radiation—from both the war and the increased levels of ultraviolet light. As a result, many of those who have survived so far will die.

Others will continue to starve. Few will be able to get sufficient supplies to survive while the new crops grow, *if* any grow. The problem won't be just in finding things to eat, but also in finding things to eat that won't add to the already dangerously high level of radioactivity in your body.

For the next five years or so there will be the constant danger of radiation contamination. Everything you eat or drink is contaminated at least partially, although maybe not so much as to bring back radiation sickness, or to mutate your crops beyond use.

You worry that the danger will continue for decades to come. After all, the reason the sky is clearing is that those particles tossed into the atmosphere are falling. The radioactivity level of the particles has decreased over time, but has it decreased enough?

It's difficult to breathe the rarefied air, and there are still enough poisonous fumes around to make breathing even more uncomfortable—and riskier. You know that this condition will also continue, possibly for the rest of your life. Unless enough of the plants of the world have managed to survive the forced hibernation of the nuclear winter, and manage to "come back" now, the oxygen cycle will never recover.

If you have children—assuming that you can find a mate who has also survived—they may or may not be whole. Genetic damage caused by massive doses of radiation are possible, and will likely have at least minor effects. It's possible that those effects will be major—infants stillborn or infants who survive birth but who can't survive the world. There is also the danger of genetic damage in generations to come.

There's an even greater chance that, even though you've survived so far, sooner or later you'll experience the damaging effects of radiation. Survivors will exhibit increased incidences of cancer, particularly leukemia, liver ailments, and a variety of other health problems.

Still, what can you do but continue to fight for survival? If you give up, or if your efforts fail, or if the aftereffects of the war have ruined any and all chances for recovery, the results will be the same.

Most of the plants and animals now are gone. Extinct. The human race is facing the same fate. All that remains are a few survivors scattered here and there around the world, but they have no way to contact each other, or to help one another.

Your little community of ten survivors could be the last of its kind on earth. A few years from now even your own group might be gone, unless all of you are unusually tough.

A Better Viewpoint

If the elements of nuclear winter aren't nearly so severe, conditions will be quite different. For example, one of the major causes of a nuclear winter would be the massive firestorms that could sweep through the cities and forests. However, during the winter, or during the wet season, those fires will be less severe. This means in turn that the nuclear winter would be less severe.

There are some who even claim that a nuclear winter won't happen at all, or, if it does, it will be relatively insignificant. Those who say this point out that the nuclear-winter theory is based on guesswork and unproved assumptions.

If nuclear bombings occur in winter or are limited to less flammable targets, the amount of smoke and soot will be greatly reduced, as will the severity and length of a nuclear winter.

If the nuclear warfare occurs over a longer period of time the severity of nuclear winter could be lessened. The destruction brought about by massive bombing runs during World War II wasn't all that different from the destruction of either of the first atom bombs. The more conventional bombing runs killed hundreds of thousands of people, leveled cities, and caused firestorms.

If the use of nuclear warheads is limited—in number, in the kind(s) of targets, and also in the time between attacks—the atmosphere will have a better chance to recover.

The Optimistic Viewpoint

A report from FEMA on civilian survival (1978) suggested that the survival rate can be quite high. For example, the population of New York City could be saved by evacuation away from that prime target area to the safer areas in the northern part of the state. However, to do this, the government would have to conscript more than half of all airliners in the country to move about 40 percent of the population of that city. The remaining 60 percent would evacuate by other means, such as private cars. Even then, total evacuation would take more than three days.

Any such evacuation would succeed only if the population obeys and follows evacuation orders, and remains orderly and without panic.

According to this same report, agriculture could return to normal after just 236 days. Life won't be pleasant during the first year, but if everyone worked together, the huge stockpiles of grain *could* be transported to the cities.

According to other reports, the death toll from a counterforce-only exchange might be as few as 20 million. According to the FEMA report half to three-fourths of the population might survive the direct effects of an even more major exchange.

Dr. Edward Teller believes that the number of survivors can be greatly increased with the implementation of proper civil defense. Evacuation is one part. Another part would involve coordinated efforts to supply the needed medical care for the injured and a steady source of food, water, and other supplies.

A Dreamer's Viewpoint

As frightening as is the idea of nuclear winter and the global extinction of many species (including, perhaps mankind), some scientists see in the development of this idea a deterrent to nuclear war.

If we assume that nuclear winter is a valid theory—and most accept it as a strong possibility—the idea that there can be a winner in a nuclear war becomes obsolete. Further, once the quantity threshold to trigger a nuclear winter has been reached, any additional warheads or weapons are useless.

An analogy that has been used involves two enemies locked in a room. If each enemy has a pistol (analogous to conventional weaponry), he can kill his opponent, or

his opponent can kill him, but there will be a survivor. A small explosive (analogous to a number of warheads below the threshold of nuclear winter) also will kill the opponent. Although it *could* injure the person who uses it, there could still be a survivor.

The analogy continues, with each enemy now having a stick of dynamite. This represents the threshold of nuclear winter. If either sets off that stick, it will kill the enemy but it will also kill the person who uses it. The parallel then goes on to describe that room as being filled with boxes and boxes of dynamite, with both enemies constantly bringing in more.

Once the world leaders come to accept nuclear winter as fact, it will be easier to remove all the boxes from the room, down to the last stick of dynamite, thus ending both the threat and the arms race.

Proponents of disarmament say that deterrence could be satisfied with levels of armament below the nuclear-winter threshold. Carl Sagan, among others, has suggested that we could do away with most or all of our landbased missiles, all of the airborne attack forces, and most of the submarine fleet.

What would the world be like without the threat of nuclear war? If the arms race could be halted, how would life change?

It's not difficult to find alternate uses for the hundreds of billions spent each year on defense. There could be a drastic reduction in taxes, for example. Invest $100 billion per year in medical research and perhaps many

It is optimistically predicted that in the event of a nuclear attack, New York City could be evacuated in about three days—if people obey orders and do not panic!

of the deadly and debilitating diseases could be cured. Another $100 billion per year could be put into space research, allowing us in a very short time to start colonizing the solar system and mining the asteroids. Some scientists claim that this would greatly reduce or even eliminate pollution, would reduce or eliminate the lack of raw materials and resources on earth, and would make it possible to develop new technologies and materials.

An official United States policy used to further justify the arms race is that it is pushing the Soviet Union into bankruptcy. Without the arms race, both the United States and the Soviet Union would have a more flourishing economy. Some "dreamers" even claim that if this happened the need for warfare would cease.

An argument often used against disarmament is that the arms race creates jobs. To combat this point, studies show that defense spending is one of the least efficient means for employment.

A 1982 study compiled by Employment Research Associates revealed that only 30 percent of Americans live in areas that benefit from defense spending.

The report went on to estimate the number of jobs created per $1 billion spent. This amount of money would create, for example, 65,000 jobs in retail trade, or 62,000 in education, or 48,000 in hospitals and medical—but just 14,000 in guided missiles and ordnance (warfare).

The Joint Congressional Economic Committee has said that the rapid buildup in defense spending is adding to the inflation rate in America. Another study, from Economic Priorities in New York, indicated that when the industrialized nations of the world are examined, those with less military expenditures show a decidedly better increase in economic growth and productivity. This study revealed that while the United States has the largest defense expenditures, it also has the lowest productivity increase, and the third lowest economic growth rate.

The Future

Many experts and world leaders tell us that we are at an important crossroads. One route, according to these people, leads to universal destruction and the end of life on earth as we know it. Another leads to something like paradise.

The trouble is that the various pathways and possibilities are blurry. No one knows for certain what will actually happen in the event of nuclear war. Nor does anyone know for sure what the results would be if disarmament became a valid possibility.

The fact that a nuclear winter is *possible* can hardly be denied. However, there is contestable evidence, on both sides, as to how it can be triggered or just how bad it would be.

Appendix:
Nukespeak

With the advent and growth of nuclear power has come an abundance of new words and terms. Many of these new words in our vocabulary are necessary scientific terms to describe something we didn't know existed before. Others have been coined by the press. Still more have been created by various agencies, governmental and private, in an effort to make things seem different from what they really are.

Another new term was "invented" just to categorize all the other new terms combined: *Nukespeak*.

Abbreviations

The use of abbreviations does several things. First, it makes more complicated phrases easier to say and write. If you were to write a report for class on intercontinental ballistic missiles, your fingers could get tired typing that phrase each time you referred to your main topic. It's much easier to use the initials, ICBM. In this way, the use of abbreviations works as a shorthand.

Second, by using initials it can make the user seem more "in the know" and more sophisticated. It might seem impressive to some to hear someone say, "I'm going to do a report on the MX and ABM projects, and their effects on C-cubed, based on studies from FEMA and the AEC."

Third, and related to the above, the use of initials and abbreviations is useful to hide the true meaning and impact of certain concepts. MUF by itself sounds like something to keep you warm in the winter; at worst it doesn't sound harmful. Material Unaccounted For, describing nuclear materials that turn up missing from various installations, sounds considerably more dangerous. The abbreviation MIRV sounds friendly enough in itself, but stands for one of the most deadly inventions in the history of the world—a multiple individually targeted reentry vehicle, of a single missile with the capability of targeting and destroying more than one city.

A more appropriate abbreviation, perhaps, is MAD. This is an acronym for "mutually assured destruction." If one side attacks, the other will retaliate. With the existing nuclear stockpiles and placements, it is almost a certainty that both sides will be destroyed.

The Press

Writers and reporters are always looking for new and dramatic ways to describe and express things. Sometimes they attempt to use "word pictures," or words that make it easier for the reader to visualize what they mean. Other times they are simply trying to drive home a particular idea or notion.

The results of the BRAVO test that took place in the Pacific in the early 1950s showed an explosive force that was far more powerful than originally predicted. It also showed that some of the fears of radioactive fallout had actually been understated.

The area had been cleared of people and vessels that could be affected by the blast. Despite the precautions taken, a Japanese fishing vessel, *The Lucky Dragon,* was a little too close. The blast wasn't a problem, but a cloud of radioactivity contaminated the fishermen and their catch.

Radioactive fallout came to be known as "ashes of death." The fish aboard *The Lucky Dragon* caused a considerable clicking when tested with a geiger counter. Due to this sound, the press dubbed them as "crying fish."

The word "priesthood" has been used over the centuries to talk about a secret or exclusive group. With the growth of nuclear armaments, and the abundance of new jargon developed, both "scientific priesthood" and "technical priesthood" have been used to describe the inner circles of those who study and work in that field. "Military priesthood" was sometimes used in a more derogatory fashion to describe those in the military who try to keep all the secrets and controls to themselves.

The Military

At the beginning of the arms race, there was a fear that the Soviet Union would build more missiles than would the United States. This came to be called "the missile gap." If they build ten new weapons, and we build only eight, the missile gap widens by two, according to the use of the terminology. It was used to convince Congress, and the American public in general, that more weapons and launching systems needed to be funded and developed.

During President Reagan's term, a new phrase was developed. This was "window of vulnerability," used primarily to describe the inability to deter the Soviet Union from starting a nuclear war. It indicated that there might be holes or gaps in our defenses through which the Soviets could achieve a victory.

All through the disarmament talks, the negotiators made use of "bargaining chips," as if each side had a box full of poker chips that could be tossed out or traded to better come to a mutual agreement. Those bargaining chips were usually considered to be weapons or systems, existent or under development. Some sources have used the same term to describe the "trading" of targeted cities, although this use of the term is generally thought to be inaccurate.

As the arms race continued, a new way to describe that race was needed. Instead of saying that a country was building more weapons, it was said to be using a "vertical proliferation." As more countries developed nuclear weapons of their own, this was "horizontal proliferation."

New countries that developed their own nuclear weapons became members of the "nuclear club." Those countries that didn't have such weapons, but which were under the protection of one of the superpowers that did, were under the "nuclear umbrella."

Along with new scenarios of attack and defense came a number of terms. Planning out these scenarios came to be called "war games."

New terms were developed to discuss the kinds of attacks, and the kinds of targets. To successfully attack a target was said to be to "crack" that target. To aim a warhead or other weapon at a specific site, and to destroy that site, came to be known as a "surgical strike." That target had then been "taken out."

When it was discovered that a nuclear explosion also brought a massive burst of electromagnetic radiation—one capable of destroying the electronic circuits of communications equipment and computers—efforts were made to "harden" military targets. This hardening helped to prevent the EMP (electromagnetic pulse) from disabling the electronics of the target.

Soon the targets came to be known as either "hard" or "soft." "Hard targets" are ones of military importance, particularly those that have the special shielding to protect the equipment, and land-based missile silos. A "soft target" is one that is unprotected, such as one of civilian importance. Drop a warhead on a missile silo to destroy that missile and prevent its launch, and you are "cracking" a "hard target." Blow up downtown Phoenix and you have cracked a "soft target."

The descriptive terminology has continued to grow. Attacking a military target and knocking out the retaliatory capability is "counter force." Attacking a civilian target, and destroying property and lives is "counter value," or "collateral damage."

There are two parts of a battle. There is the offense (attack) and the defense (retaliation). One of the strategic alternatives is to attack the enemy in such a way as to make defense or retaliation an impossibility. This is the "preemptive first strike," sometimes called a "splendid first strike."

New weapons have been developed, and along with them new words. After a more thorough study of fallout, bombs that generated less of this aftereffect were called "humanitarian bombs" or "clean bombs." Those weapons, such as the neutron bomb, that had less destructive force but which killed more people via radiation were given the name "enhanced radiation devices."

Even the way of talking about the number of casualties has changed. In previous wars the death toll could be counted quickly and easily. It has been predicted that the deaths caused by nuclear warfare wouldn't number in the thousands per day, as previously, but in the millions. Deaths are now tallied as megadeaths—millions of deaths.

Code Words

For military secrecy, many projects (and items of study within those projects) are assigned code words. There has to be some way to refer to that project and its parts without letting "the enemy" find out what is going on.

A prime example of this was the Manhattan Project.

This atomic energy project was surrounded with more secrecy than had ever been used before. Words involving nuclear science, like fission and fusion, were restricted in order to keep the enemy (and the general public) confused.

Within the project, the scientists were instructed to use special codes when referring to almost everything. "Top" was used instead of atom; "topic" was used for atomic. The word for a bomb was "boat," making a "topic boat" an atomic bomb. When fission occurs, the atom splits, or is smashed. Since they didn't want to talk about smashing, they talked about "spinning," Atom smashing becoming "top spinning."

"Urchin" was used to talk about uranium. Uranium fission became "urchin fashion," and an isotope of uranium came to be known as an "igloo of urchin." The igloo of urchin responsible for the atomic bomb is U-235. To describe this isotope the special code word "tenure" was used (two plus three plus five equals ten, with the -ure for uranium).

Fancy and Misleading Words

President Reagan, in response to increasing public and political pressure to "freeze" (stop building) or reduce the number of nuclear weapons, began to talk about a plan to "build down" (continue building new weapons, but primarily to replace older, out-of-date systems).

Many groups were (and are) still against any use of nuclear weapons, and nuclear power in general. Governmental offices and private concerns did everything they could to convince these groups that the use of nuclear power was necessary. When this didn't work, they began to describe the antinuclear attitude as an "abnormal emotional response." The same term was used to talk about the fears expressed by the general public, particularly after an accident at a nuclear power plant.

To help convince more people of the necessity for nuclear power, public relations groups were told to find "palatable synonyms" so that the dangers of nuclear power (in particular) and nuclear weapons didn't sound quite so bad.

As publicity increased, more and more people feared the possibility of a nuclear war. They knew what it was, and what it could do. So it was called something different—"radiological warfare."

In a sense, the name of the Department of War was changed to make it more palatable. Up to and through World War II this was its descriptive and apt name. With the advent of nuclear weapons, and the possibility that no one would survive the next world war, the name was changed. No one wanted to think about war, especially after the devastation of World War II. Ever since 1948 the Department of War has been, officially, the Department of Defense. This is one of those new terms that can be both misleading (since the department deals only with the subject of warfare) and more highly descriptive and accurate (since the primary concern is to defend our country from war).

As you read through this section, you came across a number of palatable synonyms. A single megadeath is easier to take than a million deaths. Collateral damage sounds better than saying that you're destroying people's homes, businesses, and lives. A surgical strike gives an almost curative sense to the total destruction of a city.

Glossary

ABCC: Atomic Bomb Casualty Commission—a group studying the long-term effects of nuclear attack, concentrating on the survivors of Hiroshima and Nagasaki.

ABM: antiballistic missile.

Abnormal emotional response: a term sometimes used to describe the attitudes and reactions of those who are against the use of nuclear power.

ACDA: Arms Control and Disarmament Agency (United States).

AEC: Atomic Energy Commission.

Airburst: a nuclear detonation that takes place far above the ground in order to cause maximum damage over a maximum range, such as over a city.

ALCM: air-launched cruise missile.

Arms race: the steady buildup of nuclear and other arms, primarily between the United States and Soviet Union, with each side trying to equal or beat the other.

Ashes of death: fallout.

Balance of terror: equal nuclear armament on opposing sides.

Bargaining chip: a weapon, weapon system, or other items that can be used in peace talks; something that can be taken away if the other side gives away something of theirs.

BRAVO: a 15-megaton testing in the Pacific. The fallout caused contamination of the catch, and radiation sickness in the 23-member crew, of a Japanese fishing boat.

Build down: a term used to describe building only enough nuclear weapons to replace those in existence, such as with better and/or more advanced devices.

C^3: command, control, and communications—Primary targets and the primary areas to defend.

C^3I: command, control, communications, and intelligence.

Clean bomb: a bomb with destructive power but relatively little radiation.

CLWEF: Council for Livable World Education Fund.

Cold War: a conflict between nations without actual warfare.

Collateral damage: destruction of civilian targets and the death of the people.

Counterforce: an attack directed against an enemy's military targets.

Countervalue: an attack directed against an enemy's cities, industry, and population.

Crack a target: to successfully strike a target with a nuclear weapon.

CTB: Comprehensive Test Ban.

Decapitation: a strike at a country's political and military leadership.

Device: bomb.

DOE: Department of Energy.

EMP: electromagnetic pulse; describes the effect of a nuclear explosion that generates enough power in the radio wave band to knock out communications.

A military or other site that has been built to resist this effect is said to be "EMP hardened."

Enhanced radiation device: the neutron bomb, designed to emit large amounts of radiation to kill people, but with relatively little damage to property.

ENUWAR: a study of the environmental consequences of a nuclear war.

ERDA: Energy Research and Development Administration.

Fallout: radioactive particles returning to earth after a nuclear explosion.

Fat Man: the second atomic bomb; exploded over Nagasaki, Japan on August 9, 1945.

FEMA: Federal Emergency Management Agency; the federal agency responsible for the planning for national disasters.

Firestorm: a fire that burns out of control from a violent rushing in of superheated air, and then combines with other fires and creates an enormous updraft.

Ground burst: a nuclear detonation near the ground. Used to "crack a hard target."

Harden: to build so that a nuclear explosion has less effect on the target, particularly from EMPs that could knock out communications.

Hard target: a target with military importance, particularly a missile silo or other protected site. (See also "Soft target" and "Hardened.")

Horizontal proliferation: more countries building nuclear arms and weapons. (See *Vertical proliferation.*)

Humanitarian Bomb: a nuclear bomb that creates a minimum of radioactive fallout; also called a "clean bomb."

ICBM: intercontinental ballistic missile.

ICSU: International Council of Scientific Unions.

Iron Curtain: isolation of Eastern Europe by the Soviet Union. The term was coined by Winston Churchill.

Kilo-: prefix meaning "thousand." A kiloton is a thousand tons.

Little Boy: the first atomic bomb; exploded over Hiroshima, Japan on August 6, 1945.

LOW: launch-on-warning; the "use them or lose them" idea.

LTBT: Limited Test Ban Treaty. Sometimes seen as just LTB, for Limited Test Ban; or TBT or Test Ban Treaty.

MAD: mutually assured destruction.

Manhattan Project: code name for the first atomic bomb project in America.

Mass fire: a number of smaller fires combining into a single, larger fire.

MBFR: mutual and balanced force reductions.

Mega-: prefix meaning "million." A megaton is an explosive force equivalent to that of a million tons of TNT.

Megadeath: millions of deaths. An attack resulting in 1 megadeath translates to mean 1 million people have died.

MIKE: project for the first testing of a hydrogen bomb.

MIRV: multiple independently targetable reentry vehicle.

MUF: material unaccounted for. Describes nuclear material, mostly enriched uranium and plutonium, missing from stock, particularly from nuclear energy generating sites.

NCAR: National Center for Atmospheric Research.

NRC: National Research Council.

NRDC: Natural Resources Defense Council.

Nuclear club: nations of the world with nuclear weapons.

Nuclear exchange: nuclear war.

Nuclear umbrella: a less powerful nation being protected by a more powerful nation with a threat of the use of nuclear weapons against attackers.

OTA: Office of Technology Assessment.

Overkill: more killing potential in the nuclear weapon stockpile than there are people to kill.

Overpressure: the air being driven outwards from the center of a nuclear blast.

Ozone: a thin layer in the upper atmosphere of our planet that blocks ultraviolet light.

Preemptive first strike: an initial attack designed to destroy an enemy so that the enemy cannot retaliate.

Priesthood: a term coined by Alvin Weinberg to describe the special group of people, either technological or military, who should have long-term control of nuclear energy.

Pyrotoxins: poisonous fumes released in a fire, such as from a city burning as a result of a nuclear explosion.

Rad: a unit of measure of radiation, with 1 rad being equivalent to 10^9 (1,000,000,000) particles per square centimeter.

Rem: the standard unit of measurement of absorbed radiation in living tissue, adjusted so that one rem of any radiation will produce the same biological effect.

Radiological warfare: nuclear war.

SAC: Strategic Air Command.

SALT: strategic arms limitation talks.

SAM: surface-to-air missile.

SCOPE: Scientific Committee on Problems of the Environment.

SDI: Strategic Defense Initiative: more commonly called "Star Wars." Represents a system of weapons in space meant to shoot down incoming missiles.

SLBM: submarine-launched ballistic missile.

Soft target: a target without military importance; a civilian target.

Splendid first strike: same as "preemptive first strike."

SRAM: short-range attack missile.

Star Wars: common name for the Strategic Defense Initiative (SDI).

Sunshine unit: a term used by the AEC to measure fallout, comparing the radioactivity of strontium-90 to normal calcium.

Surgical strike: an attack that completely destroys a target, particularly a city.

Synergism: cooperative action of several forces that has a total effect that is greater than the sum of the effects taken separately.

Thermal radiation: the heat produced in a nuclear blast—approximately 35 percent of the total released energy.

Tinkerbell effect: a term coined by FEMA to describe the attitude of many people who believe that a national emergency will not happen.

TTAPS: the most widely accepted model used to predict the effects of nuclear winter. The initials stand for the scientists who developed the model—Richard P. Turco, O. Brian Toon, Thomas P. Ackerman, James B. Pollack and Carl Sagan.

Vertical proliferation: more nuclear arms and weapons being built within a country. (See *Horizontal proliferation.*)

War games: nuclear war scenarios worked out, usually by computer.

WHO: World Health Organization.

X + 1: the idea that for however many weapons your enemy has, you must have one more; and then he must have one more; then you must have one more; and so on.

For Further
Reading

Adams, Ruth and Cullen, Sue, eds. *The Final Epidemic: Physicians and Scientists on Nuclear War.* Chicago: Educational Foundation for Nuclear Science, 1982.

Andrews, Elaine K. *Civil Defense in the Nuclear Age.* New York: Franklin Watts, 1985.

Cracraft, James. *The Soviet Union Today: An Interpretive Guide.* Chicago: University of Chicago Press, 1983.

Ehrlich, Paul R. *The Cold and the Dark: The World After Nuclear War.* New York: W.W. Norton, 1984.

Ford, Daniel et al. *Beyond the Freeze: The Road to Nuclear Sanity.* Boston: Beacon Press, 1982.

Harwell, Mark A. *Nuclear Winter.* New York: Springer-Verlag, 1984.

Kaplan, Fred. *The Wizards of Armageddon: Strategists of the Nuclear Age.* Simon and Schuster, 1983.

Kennan, George F. *The Nuclear Delusion: Soviet-American Relations in the Atomic Age.* New York: Pantheon, 1983.

Leaning, Jennifer and Keyes, Langley, eds. *The Counterfeit Ark: Crisis Relocation for Nuclear War.* Cambridge, MA: Ballinger Publishing, 1983.

Scoville, Herbert, Jr. *The MX: Prescription for Disaster.* Cambridge, MA: MIT Press, 1981.

Taylor, L.B., Jr. *The Nuclear Arms Race.* New York: Franklin Watts, 1982.

For Further
Information

Council for a Livable World
Education Fund (CLWEF)
11 Beacon Street
Boston, Massachusetts 02108

National Resources
Defense Council (NRDC)
1350 New York Ave. NW.
Suite 300
Washington, D.C. 20005

Bulletin of Atomic Scientists
5801 S. Kenwood
Chicago, Illinois 60637

National Research Council
2101 Constitution Ave.
Washington, D.C. 20418

Index